THE ODYSSEY

The Odyssey

A DRAMATIC RETELLING OF HOMER'S EPIC

SIMON ARMITAGE

W. W. NORTON & COMPANY

NEW YORK LONDON

First published in 2006 by Faber and Faber Limited
3 Queen Square London WC1N 3AU

For information about permission to reproduce selections from this book,
write to Permissions, W. W. Norton & Company, Inc., 500 Fifth Avenue,
New York, NY 10110

For information about special discounts for bulk purchases, please contact
W. W. Norton Special Sales at specialsales@wwnorton.com or 800-233-4830

Manufacturing by Courier Westford
Production manager: Devon Zahn

Library of Congress Cataloging-in-Publication Data

Armitage, Simon, 1963–
[Homer's Odyssey]
The odyssey : a dramatic retelling of Homer's epic / Simon Armitage.
— 1st American ed.
p. cm.
Previously published as: Homer's Odyssey.
ISBN 978-0-393-33081-6 (pbk.)
1. Odysseus (Greek mythology)—Fiction. 2. Penelope (Greek
mythology)—Fiction. 3. Poseidon (Greek deity)—Fiction.
I. Homer. Odyssey. II. Title.
PR6051.R564H66 2008
822'.914—dc22

2008001290

W. W. Norton & Company, Inc.
500 Fifth Avenue, New York, N.Y. 10110
www.wwnorton.com

W. W. Norton & Company Ltd.,
Castle House, 75/76 Wells Street, London W1T 3QT

1 2 3 4 5 6 7 8 9 0

INTRODUCTION

Twenty years have passed since Odysseus sailed away to wage war against the Trojans, leaving behind his beloved wife, Penelope, and Telemachus, their infant son. The conflict itself lasts for ten of those years, but another decade of strife awaits the victorious Odysseus as he hauls home towards his kingdom of Ithaca. The *Odyssey* is the story of that homeward journey, a journey which tests the resources and strength of its hero to breaking point. In his way stand cannibals and whirlpools, witches and ghosts, monsters and Gods. The battles he must win are battles of the body, the mind and the spirit. Homer's *Odyssey* forms part of the bedrock of all written art; one of the first ever works of literature, it is a triumph of intellectual, imaginative and technical genius. Ultimately, though, it is a story, and for all its evocation of the supernatural and the otherworldly, it is a story of humankind. At its heart is a family – a husband, wife and son – desperate to reunite and determined to survive.

This dramatization was commissioned by BBC Radio 4 and broadcast over a weekend in late summer, 2004. Much of Homer's *Odyssey* is written as narrated poem, and when characters do enter into discourse, it tends to be with formal speech, rather than what we might call dialogue. Faced with that situation, the role of the dramatist is to transform such narration into a series of conversations and exchanges, and to actualize some of its unspoken intentions by putting speech into characters' mouths. In other words, to get people to talk. It would be impossible, not to mention pointless, to perform such a transformation without running a few risks and taking a few liberties. And yet the version presented here hopes never to stray *too* far from the content, chronology and atmosphere of the original. It is not set in a housing estate in Salford. It does not depict the Achaeans as veterans of the Gulf War or asylum-seekers, though of course we should not be surprised if the *Odyssey* rings with echoes and resonances of our contemporary world. Such is the power and purpose of myth.

My thanks are due to Janet Whittaker for conceiving and directing this project, and for having the honesty to tell me that two other authors initially associated with the commission subsequently passed away. Tackling these colossal old texts is a huge and daunting undertaking. On delivery of the final manuscript, I wrote on the final page, 'Can I die now?' Many thanks also to Peter Jones for his advice and comments. Finally, I owe a huge debt of gratitude to those ranks of scholars and authors, some of whom spent a lifetime translating the *Odyssey* from a twelve-thousand-line, two-and-a-half-thousand-year-old epic into the contemporary literature of their day. Of the modern translations, those by E. V. Rieu, Richmond Lattimore and Robert Fagles have inspired and illuminated the most.

One more thing. Although this version of the *Odyssey* was developed as a radio play and is presented here in script form, it was always in the back of my mind that it should have a further life as a piece of writing. Not just something to be performed, but something to read. A book, in fact.

Simon Armitage

Remind us, Muse, of that man of many means,
sent spinning the length and breadth of the map
after bringing the towers of Troy to their knees;

of the lessons he learned in the cities of great minds,
and the heartbreak he suffered, roaming the seas
to land his shipmates and salvage his life.

But for all the torture and grief he sustained
his comrades were lost; heedless fools,
they gorged on the flesh of the Cattle of the Sun.
In turn, the God of the Sun made death their domain.

Muse, daughter of Memory and Zeus,
where to start this story is yours to choose.

I

OLYMPUS

A council of the Gods. A dozen or so voices are chattering amongst themselves.

ZEUS

What I say is this:
Odysseus must be punished.
Poseidon must have his revenge.

General agreement amongst the Gods.

ATHENA

But why, father? This man was a hero at Troy.
One of our favourites.

ZEUS

We owe him no special favour.
He's a human in the end. A mortal.

ATHENA

There's no shame in being human.

ZEUS

They stumble from one tragedy to the next,
never improving, never learning from their mistakes,
then blame us for their frailties and faults.
Their misfortunes are their own!
Our words of warning fall on deaf ears
and they turn a blind eye to our signs.
When we send eagles
to signal our thoughts in the sky,
what do they do – stand and point and stare,
like . . . birdwatchers!

After all these years you'd expect some change,
some progress, some development – some sense.
But their behaviour gets worse.
They are children, squabbling brats,
and the world is their kindergarten.

ATHENA

There are always exceptions to the rule, aren't there,
    father?

ZEUS

And exceptions that prove it as well.

ATHENA

All I'm saying is . . . we shouldn't be so quick to judge.
Take each case on its merits. See the person,
not just the species as a whole. Consider the man.

ZEUS

Consider Odysseus – that's what you mean, isn't it?
Speak up, child.

ATHENA

Well, yes, he's an example of the kind of thing I'm talking
    about.

Groans from the other Gods.

ATHENA (*stridently*)

His predicament is a shadow on my heart
and grows darker every day.

It's only yesterday you Gods were cheering him on.
Praising his cunning and skill, toasting the way
he conjured victory out of defeat at Troy,
imagined a hollow horse made from a ship's beams.

HERMES

His savages butchered and ate the Cattle of the Sun – those
beautiful, lumbering bulls that never hurt anyone.

ATHENA

That's rich coming from you.
You – the world's first cattle rustler.
Fifty heifers, wasn't it, stolen from Apollo?

HERMES

I was an infant. It was a prank.
I gave forty-eight of them back.

ATHENA

I thought you of all people would be more sympathetic.
You – the God of Travellers, the Light in the Dark.

HERMES

I helped him once. I pointed out the moly flower,
saved him from being magicked into a hog.

ATHENA

That was years ago. He's still lost.

HERMES

Is it my job to hold his hand all the way home?

ATHENA

Do you have some more important task?

HERMES

Well, I . . .

ATHENA

Don't expect fires to be lit or bulls to be slaughtered
in your name, if the prayers of a struggling traveller
fall on deaf ears. Don't expect temples and grottoes.

HERMES
   My image appears by every path,
   in every roadside shrine.

ATHENA
   Roads and paths alter their course. Humans have fickle
      hearts.

HERMES
   It isn't a popularity contest.

ATHENA
   You'll be forgotten. Wiped from memory.

HERMES
   Ridiculous.

ATHENA
   You won't exist.

HERMES (*after a few moments of thought*)
   I suppose a little nudge in the right direction wouldn't
      hurt.

ZEUS
   Odysseus blinded the Cyclops. Seared his only eye with a
      burning branch.
   The Cyclops. Poseidon's son. My nephew no less!

ATHENA
   Put yourself in Odysseus' shoes and tell me how it feels.
   Twenty years away from his land . . .

ANOTHER GOD (*pipes up*)
   Nineteen.

ATHENA
   Ten years fighting and winning the war at Troy,

[8]

ten more making his journey home,
seven of those snared in Calypso's net.
Calypso, who charms him with voodoo words,
encircles him with her legs,
blows mumbo-jumbo into his ears to make him forget.
But he doesn't forget.
He dreams of the fires of Ithaca,
scans the horizon for smoke,
weeps for his people, his wife and his son.
And after all the sacrifices he made in your name, father.
I don't know how you sleep.

ZEUS
Yes, true, he's suffered more than most, but . . .

ATHENA
And his tired wife, Penelope, who waits.

ZEUS
Penelope, yes, she's patient to the last.

ATHENA
And Telemachus, his son. A young man now
who was only a babe in arms when his father's boat
sailed out of the bay.

ZEUS
True. A crying shame.

ATHENA
And the loyal people of his home town . . .

ZEUS
All right. ALL RIGHT!
No one forgets proud Odysseus,
stuck there on some forsaken rock in Calypso's web.

But my brother Poseidon harbours a deep grudge.
He wants blood.

ATHENA (*with obvious flattery*)
Father. Father . . . most noble Zeus . . .

ZEUS
On the other hand, no one would deny the man a fighting
chance.

The Gods mumble and grumble amongst themselves.

ZEUS (*whispering*)
Well, Athena. Here's your moment. What do you suggest?

ATHENA (*struggling to make herself heard*)
Dispatch Hermes to that bewitching nymph,
tell her to untangle Odysseus from her spell.
Let him sail home under a stiff breeze.

ZEUS (*angry*)
You'll do me the honour of listening to Zeus' daughter.

Silence in the hall.

Hermes, fly off to that bewitching nymph,
tell her to untangle Odysseus from her spell.
Let him sail home under a stiff breeze.
He can take his chances on the high sea.

All the Gods shall unite and agree.

Murmurings of dissent from the Gods.

(*with great thunder*)
ZEUS HAS SPOKEN. ALL THE GODS SHALL AGREE.

Silence. Then the Gods disperse. In agreement.

ATHENA

My father, mightiest of the mighty,
highest among the high . . .

ZEUS

That's enough worming and wheedling for one day.
And what part shall you play in all this?

ATHENA

I'll go to Ithaca with a plan.
Light a fire in the mind of Telemachus, Odysseus' only
    son,
put fuel in his thoughts.

ZEUS

Why such haste?
After twenty years, is there any need to rush?

ATHENA

For us immortals, time is a circle that never ends.
But man has a fistful of sand and treasures every grain.

ZEUS

You are your father's daughter, no doubt of that.

ATHENA

I'll take this spear. Disguise myself as Mentes,
an old friend of Odysseus.
I'll appear as a man – in the flesh.

ITHACA. THE PALACE OF ODYSSEUS.

The suitors are drinking, feasting and playing games. They throw dice, arm-wrestle and occasionally break out into bawdy songs.

ANTINOUS
More wine over here.

EURYMACHUS
And the good stuff from the far cellar, mind.
Not the piss you keep for unwanted guests.
And more pig.
Succulent suckling pig with its crackling skin.

AMPHINOMUS
Steady on a bit. There's no need to go over the top.

ANTINOUS
Let him talk.

EURYMACHUS
And its tender roll of loin . . .
And its supple flanks . . .

And its virgin balls . . .

ANTINOUS
Speaking of which, here comes our host.
(*to Telemachus*)
Telemachus, a delicious feast again.
Your kitchen does you proud.

TELEMACHUS
Never let it be said that you starved.

EURYMACHUS
> And the wine – quite delicious.
> Zeus himself would smile at the taste.

TELEMACHUS
> If there's any left when you're finished
> I'll be glad to offer him a glass.

> You'll have to excuse me, though.
> A visitor stands in the door,
> another stranger I'll make welcome in my father's house.

ANTINOUS
> Be my guest.

The suitors laugh behind his back as Telemachus walks away.

TELEMACHUS (*wearily*)
> One more mouth to feed. Well, don't stand in the porch.

MENTES (*Athena in disguise*)
> Not the most heartfelt welcome I've ever had.

TELEMACHUS
> We never turn our back on visitors,
> but you suitors are eating us out of house and home.
> Don't expect to be welcomed with open arms.

MENTES
> I'm no suitor.
> I'm Mentes, a friend of your father's from a long way
>   back.

TELEMACHUS (*eagerly*)
> You have news of my father? Where is he?
> Has he sent you ahead to announce his arrival?

MENTES

No news like that I'm afraid.

TELEMACHUS

Then what brings you to Ithaca?

MENTES

I'm . . . anchored in the bay with my men,
en route to Temese to trade metal and ore.
I stopped in to pay my respects.

Bawdy singing rises in the background.

MENTES

Forgive me, but this is a scandal.
What gives those men the right to behave like swine
in the house of noble Odysseus?

TELEMACHUS

Let's step outside for some fresh air as we talk.

They go outside.

Two decades ago my father sailed out of view
and we haven't set eyes on him since.
For years and years I imagined him standing
where you stood just moments ago,
filling the frame of the door,
back to throw his arms around his family
and claim his house.
But now I fear the worst.

MENTES

A man like Odysseus wouldn't just disappear without
trace.

TELEMACHUS

I have a nightmare vision when I close my eyes.
My father, dead and alone on some stony plain,
or deep in an ocean trench. He's water now, or he's dust.

MENTES

You sound like you've given up hope.

TELEMACHUS

And there's more pain to bear:
these men that lounge on his rugs
and loaf at his hearth,
grazing and gulping their way through our wealth,
these 'suitors' lay claim to my mother's heart.
But because my father has no tomb or grave
she can't say no and she can't say yes.
So they gorge themselves at our expense
and we feed them on silver plates.
We're besieged, from inside our own house!

MENTES

Telemachus, listen to me. I'm no teller of fortunes
and I can't read the meaning of birds in the sky.
But the Gods have put a thought in my mind;
for your own sake you should act on what I say.

I believe these suitors will shriek for forgiveness before
        they die.

TELEMACHUS

It's a mouth-watering thought. If I were more of a
        man . . .

MENTES

Get a boat of twenty oars.
Sail to Pylos then Sparta,

seek news of your father from his friends.
They'll tell you of the glorious victory at Troy.
They'll inspire you. You'll grow with every word.

TELEMACHUS
No, they'll meet me on the pier, awkward in grief,
like distant uncles consoling a dead man's son,
saying how sorry they were to hear of my loss.
Then I'll be crushed.

MENTES
If you hear of his death
then heap stones on a plot of earth
and call it his grave.
Then your mother Penelope must choose her groom.

But if you hear word that he lives,
sail back to Ithaca, and hold yourself proud and straight.

TELEMACHUS
You speak with a fatherly tone.

MENTES
You're no longer a child, Telemachus.
It's time to prove that to yourself.
Now go back inside. I'll make myself scarce.

TELEMACHUS
Wait . . .

Athena leaves.

My father had friends in high places,
friends of unusual nature, other-worldly . . .

*The voices of the suitors rise again. Over them comes the
voice of a minstrel, Phemios.*

PHEMIOS (*sings*)
> *How many boats for Helen of Troy?*
> *How many boats, how many boats,*
> *How many trees were cut to their knees*
> *to bring her back over the ocean?*
>
> *How many weapons for Helen of Troy?*
> *How many arrows, how many spears,*
> *how many sorrows and how many tears*
> *to bring her back over the ocean?*
>
> *How many miles for Helen of Troy?*
> *How many miles, how many miles,*
> *how many days in the wild of the waves*
> *to bring her back over the ocean?*
>
> *How many soldiers for Helen of Troy?*
> *How much force and how much blood,*
> *how many foals from a horse made of wood*
> *to bring her back over the ocean?*
>
> *How many lives for Helen of Troy?*
> *How many lives, how many lives,*
> *how many husbands and how many wives*
> *to bring her back over the ocean?*

Penelope appears at the head of the stairs. The room falls
silent. The minstrel's song grinds to a halt.

ANTINOUS
Penelope. You grace us with your presence.

EURYMACHUS
You honour us.

AMPHINOMUS
Here's a seat by the fire, and a cloak for your shoulders.

PENELOPE
    It was music that stirred me.

PHEMIOS
    Thank you, my lady.

PENELOPE
    Troubled me, I mean.
    Roused me out of the comfort of sleep.
    Have you only the one song?

PHEMIOS
    No, lady. Thousands.

PENELOPE
    Then sing another. Not the song of Troy.
    It climbed my stairs, rising like smoke,
    seeping under the door and bringing me to tears.
    Let me sleep. I'm tired.

Penelope retires. The suitors mutter amongst themselves.

EURYMACHUS
    She's an icy one.

ANTINOUS
    She'll melt.

EURYMACHUS
    I know what I'd be like after twenty years with my legs
        crossed.
    I'd be at boiling point.

AMPHINOMUS
    Beautiful, though. Standing there at the head of the stairs.
    Against the evening light.

EURYMACHUS
  She takes her wedding vows too seriously.
  She takes her fidelity too far.

AMPHINOMUS
  That's why we want her, isn't it?
  That's why we're queuing up for her hand.
  We want that faithfulness for ourselves.

EURYMACHUS
  And everything that comes with it.

ANTINOUS
  Property.

EURYMACHUS
  Weaponry.

ANTINOUS
  Lakes of wine.

EURYMACHUS
  Herds of cattle.

ANTINOUS
  Gold.

EURYMACHUS
  Fame.

AMPHINOMUS
  My intentions are entirely honourable.

EURYMACHUS
  So are mine. It's just that I've got some very big
    intentions!

ANTINOUS

It's like a land of plenty waiting behind a locked gate.
One day she'll say yes, and give one man amongst us the
  key.
The key to paradise.
When she stood there just now,
with the sun behind her, illuminated, the last rays of dusk
making a filament of her body beneath her dress,
which of us didn't steal a glimpse of what lies ahead, on
  the other side . . .

TELEMACHUS (*furiously*)

You suitors, camped out at our expense,
gnawing your way like rats through our estate,
I'll keep you fed and watered
for as long as you stay – it's what society expects.
But if there were justice in this world,
Zeus would punish you for your gluttony,
he'd put an end to your infinite appetites,
and I for one would give him endless thanks.

EURYMACHUS (*aside*)

What's that bed-wetter whining about now?

ANTINOUS

Telemachus, what's got into you?
How dare you talk with such impertinence,
as if the Gods had given you leave to speak?

TELEMACHUS

For as long as my father Odysseus is away
I'll be lord and master in this house,
I'll be the owner of all his hard-won fortunes
and I'll speak as I please.

EURYMACHUS
   Say what you will,
   the outcome of all this lies in the lap of the Gods,
   and there's nothing you can do to alter what they decide.

ANTINOUS
   Correct.
   Anyway, who was the visitor who arrived unannounced,
   then vanished into thin air?
   Another suitor, joining the long and winding queue,
   or just a tinker pushing some second-rate goods?

TELEMACHUS
   A friend of my father's – a merchant trading shore to shore.
   He stopped to pay his respects
   but when he set his eyes on this vulgar scene
   he made his excuses and ran to catch the wind.

ANTINOUS
   That tone of voice again, Telemachus.
   Well, let me say this, if we have become debased
   there's only your mother to blame.
   There's a name for people like her.
   We could have been off in the wide world,
   lying beside any woman who took our fancy –
   but good Penelope keeps us hanging on.
   For nearly four years we've dangled on a string
   while she sends us encouraging nods and winks.
   We've invested too much time to just walk away.

TELEMACHUS
   She is a faithful mother and wife.

ANTINOUS
   She's a clever trickster as well. What was it she said to us?

'All you who flatter me
and are eager for my hand,
let me first weave this shroud
for Laertes my father-in-law,
who is frail and old.'

EURYMACHUS
'What will the womenfolk think of me
if he dies without a sheet
to wind his royal body in?'

ANTINOUS
'When the weaving's done,
when the shroud's complete,
then I'll choose a man.'

So we let her weave.
Season after season, year after year we let her weave,
until one of her maids whispered in my ear
that what she stitched by day she unpicked at night.
That's the kind of devious mind we're up against.

TELEMACHUS
She plays for time, holding out hope for my father's
return.
Who could blame her for that?

EURYMACHUS
She's a vixen. Cunning and sly.

AMPHINOMUS
Telemachus, your mother is a prize worthy of any
man . . .

ANTINOUS
Burn this into your brain, Telemachus:

we'll not give up the chase,
so the quicker you cut the apron strings
and marry her off to whichever suitor she most deserves,
the better for everyone concerned.

The door bursts open. Halitherses staggers in, breathless.

HALITHERSES
A sign in the sky.

EURYMACHUS
Who's this old bag of bones?

TELEMACHUS
Halitherses. He has a knack for reading the flight of birds.
Tell us what you saw.

HALITHERSES
Two eagles soaring over the town.

ANTINOUS
It happens every day.

HALITHERSES
They glided side by side,
then suddenly turned on each other in mid-air,
lashing out with their fearful talons,
tearing feathers with their terrible beaks, making an
    ungodly din . . .
It spells disaster for you suitors.
It means bloody misfortune is being plotted somewhere
    overhead . . .

EURYMACHUS
That's crap.
Someone take this coffin-dodger outside and leave him
    to rot.

HALITHERSES
It's not crap. There'll be ructions.

EURYMACHUS
You couldn't predict your way out of your own hat!
Save your breath, incontinent old corpse.
And here's a forecast for you: if you can find your way
    home,
tell your children what fate has in store for them
if their father keeps opening his trap.

HALITHERSES
I'm not wrong. You'll see that I'm not.

AMPHINOMUS
I know something about this kind of thing.
He's right when he says that two eagles mean trouble.

ANTINOUS
Birds do peculiar things every day of the week.
They're just birds. It's . . . ornithology.

HALITHERSES (*rather pathetically*)
I've predicted all kinds of things. I'm good at it.

ANTINOUS
You're a shit-stirrer, that's what you are.
Odysseus is as dead as stone and everyone knows it.
So why put ideas of vengeance in his son's head?
Telemachus should be left to finish his grieving,
then his mother could be married off.

TELEMACHUS
I have a proposition for you men.

EURYMACHUS
You're hardly in a position to bargain . . .

[24]

ANTINOUS
    Let him speak.

TELEMACHUS
    Allow me a ship and twenty men to row.
    I'll sail to Pylos, then on to Sparta,
    and ask for hard news of my father,
    find the man who last saw him alive
    or the man who pronounced him dead.
    If he lives, grant me another year,
    twelve months for him to find Ithaca.
    If he has perished, I'll build a tomb
    in his name, and make offerings
    in his honour, in keeping with his fame.
    Then one man here shall marry his widow.

EURYMACHUS (*hushed, under the hubbub of voices*)
    It's a trick. He's plotting our murder.

AMPHINOUS
    It seems a reasonable enough request.

EURYMACHUS
    He'll bring back an army
    or recipes for poison to mix with our supper.
    He's as slippery as his mother.

ANTINOUS
    Maybe.
    But he's young, inexperienced and full of idiot ideas.
    More likely he'll drown at sea.
    Which will make our job here a whole lot smoother.
    Whoever marries the mother could keep the house –
    the family's worldly goods we'll split between us.
    There's nothing to lose. He's played right into our hands.

(to *Telemachus*)
Very well.
Bon voyage, Telemachus:
we'll scan the waves for your safe return.

ON ITHACA'S BEACH AT NIGHT

Telemachus is alone.

TELEMACHUS
  You who came to me in my father's house,
  a Goddess in the body of a man, who set my pulse racing
  with a plan, can you hear me now?

ATHENA (*appearing out of the air*)
  Your journey waits for you, Telemachus.
  It's a test of your mind and your strength,
  and a test of your birth: prove to yourself
  that you are your father's son, that his blood
  is in your blood, and you'll journey into joy.
  Pull yourself up to your full height.
  You have a lot to live up to. Many sons
  are blocked out by their father's light;
  the bigger and stronger the parent tree,
  the weaker the stripling, standing in its shade.
  But I think you'll grow tall and straight.
  Here's a fast ship, fitted out, ready to sail.
  Collect provisions for the trip – stuff satchels
  with meal and top up the jars with strong wine.

TELEMACHUS
  The suitors seemed suspicious.
  If I return to the house they might . . .

ATHENA
  They're too busy roasting meat and swilling drink
  to bother with you. Don't lose confidence now.
  Screw your courage to a point. For my part,

I'll steal through the town recruiting the best men.
They won't say no when they see into my eyes.

Start plotting a course, Telemachus, the stars
point the way tonight, under clear, open skies.

PENELOPE'S BED-CHAMBER

Penelope half-sings, half-hums the final verse of Phemios'
Song of Troy.

EURYCLEIA
Come back from the window, my lady. There's a chill
 wind tonight.

PENELOPE
My son stands on the beach.

EURYCLEIA
Looking for signs of his father. Hopeful to the last.

PENELOPE
Two sets of footprints on the sand,
but he stands alone.

EURYCLEIA
He'll be pacing up and down. That's what I do when I'm
 nervous.

PENELOPE
And the wind blows the wrong way
for this time of night, away from the shore.

EURYCLEIA
It's a chill wind all right. Straight off the mountains.
Come away from the window now and take this cloak.

PENELOPE
Do you hear what those young men say about me?

EURYCLEIA
Take no notice.

PENELOPE

That I'm carved from ice.

EURYCLEIA

From standing at that window in a chill wind.

PENELOPE

That I give them knowing looks, feed them with hope.

EURYCLEIA

What do they know about a woman's face?

PENELOPE

That I'm the one making the situation worse.

EURYCLEIA

It's the drink in them that talks. They're loud-mouths,
and louder still with a jar of wine in their gut.

PENELOPE

It's true, though, isn't it?

EURYCLEIA

What's true?

PENELOPE

That I'm the corn that keeps the locusts fed.

EURYCLEIA

Don't torture yourself.

PENELOPE

But I'm right, aren't I?

EURYCLEIA

I'm a brusher of hair and a hanger of clothes – I'm not
paid for my wit.

PENELOPE
Yes, it's unfair of me . . .

EURYCLEIA
But since you're asking, I'll tell you how it is.
You live like a widow, with no man at your side,
and you've lived like that for nigh on twenty years.
Until you bury Odysseus, you're still his wife.
It pays to be cold on the outside
with that lot down there drooling at your feet
and sniffing under the bedroom door.
But I know you. I've known you for donkey's years,
and there's a flame somewhere inside, right?
In your heart, I shouldn't wonder, and it won't go out.

PENELOPE
Shouldn't I snuff it dead, for everyone's sake?

EURYCLEIA
No one can change what's in their own heart.
Not even a queen. And that's as much as I know on the
   topic.

PENELOPE
Maybe he's found a better pillow for his head,
next to a younger woman with silkier flesh.

EURYCLEIA
She'd have to be made from silk itself to have skin any
   silkier than yours.
I've known some skin in my time and yours is the silkiest
   of the lot.
There's skin and there's skin, and let me tell you, yours is
   pure silk.

PENELOPE

You underestimate your powers of argument.
You should sit in the council of the wise.

EURYCLEIA

Why, do they need a brusher of hair?
Now, don't be going to that window again, it's a chill
   wind
from the mountain. You'll get a ghost in your lungs.
And if that's everything I'll say goodnight.

Eurycleia leaves.

PENELOPE

Would that be so bad?
To end it, inhale a cold death?

She breathes deeply.

To join my husband on the other side,
is that what the Gods have in mind?

OLYMPUS

ZEUS

Athena, my daughter, give me a progress report.
You were a visitation in Ithaca overnight.
Are the vultures still circling the house of Odysseus?

ATHENA

They are.

ZEUS

And what of his son, young Telemachus?
Has he formulated a plan?
Has he 'hatched from the egg of his inaction?'

ATHENA

He has.

ZEUS

And is patient Penelope still faithfulness itself?

ATHENA

She is.

ZEUS

I hope you were discreet. It doesn't do to meddle too
   much.
Makes them dependent.
Makes them over-reliant upon our interventions.

ATHENA

I was subtle and tactful. I've blown a gentle breeze
into the sails of the situation – it's what was called for.
But things need a further push. Odysseus
was like a father to his people, almost Godlike;

now it's shameful to hear his friends and neighbours
speak so casually of him. His name slips from memory.
He's like a great ship that sank on its return journey,
lost and only half-remembered, under the surface.

ZEUS

At least they don't live for ever, like us. My memory –
it's like a museum. Infinite rooms, covered in dust.

ATHENA

We need to be active on all fronts.
My brother, Hermes, when will he . . .

ZEUS

Already flown. Just after dawn he collected his spear,
pulled his laces tight, and putting his best foot first
went island-hopping over the waves to Calypso's cave.
She's a crafty one, though. She won't give up her catch
just like that. Let's hope our messenger keeps his nerve.

ATHENA

She has a soft spot for Hermes. He'll talk her round.

ZEUS

She has a soft spot for Odysseus too, we might say!
And a double-jointed tongue.

Here, I'll blow a hole in the clouds. Let's watch.

CALYPSO'S ISLAND

Hermes approaches the mouth of the cave. Inside, Calypso is singing quietly to herself.

CALYPSO (*sings*)
Fountains like pillars of light
light these meadows
of wild-grown flowers and wild herbs
on the path to her cave.

The limbs of the cedar
alight in the hearth.
Sweet-smoking cedar breathes incense
out of the cave's mouth.

Vines clustered with grapes.
Leaves of the alder, sprigs of the poplar
and cypress cones litter the floor
of the cave's mouth.

Land-birds nest in the beard
of grasses and ferns
at the cave's mouth.
Overhead, seabirds mew and meep,

wheeling up and wheeling down,
riding the thermals, riding the warmth
from the cave's mouth.

HERMES (*taking up the song*)
And down in the cave itself,

out of the cave's throat,
a woman's song. A woman's voice,

fine, carried light as a thread of hair
floating on thin air.

CALYPSO

What do you want?

HERMES

Calypso, I've travelled over vast, empty plains
of the sea and there's salt on my tongue.
Before we speak, won't you offer an old friend a drink?

CALYPSO

It's true there's a common bond between us, Hermes.
I'd go further than that even – I'm fond of you.
But no one travels to this far-flung outcrop
just to marvel at the violets in the fields
or drink the fresh water – pure as it is.

HERMES

Come into the light – let me see your face.

CALYPSO

I'll help if I can, but I suspect the worst.

HERMES

You're being straightforward with me,
I respect you for that, and I'll be honest in return.
I speak to you as one God to another;
you might have chosen to live like a mortal,
earth-bound and modest, but a God is what you are.
So you know that when word comes from Olympus
it can't be ignored, and when those words
come from the mouth of Zeus himself, they're arrows of
    iron
which won't be deflected or stopped.

CALYPSO

And he fires his iron words in my direction, does he?
I can guess why.

HERMES

He says at night you sleep next to a man.
No crime in itself, except that man is Odysseus,
who fought and won the long battle for Troy
and was shipwrecked here on his voyage home.
He's been a prisoner in your keep for seven years now,
and I'm instructed to instruct you to let him go.

CALYPSO

He's no prisoner. He can leave when he likes.

HERMES

And what would he sail in, a walnut shell?

CALYPSO

He loves me! Why would he want to risk his neck?

HERMES

Well, let's ask him, shall we? Where is he now?

CALYPSO

On his favourite rock overlooking the bay.

HERMES

Looking east towards Ithaca, no doubt.

CALYPSO

He's happy. He's never tried to escape.

HERMES

That rock he sits on was visible from miles out at sea.
Bleached white, and not by the dung of birds
or the throw of the sea, but by a man's tears.

CALYPSO (*angry*)
 You Gods on your mountain perch, you're a joke.
 You're the high-priests of hypocrisy.
 When a male God swoops down on a woman
 or forces himself on some innocent young thing,
 you call it Fate. When a female God
 falls for a mortal or takes a man into her bed
 an earthquake of disapproval blows its top.

HERMES
 You're confusing politics with matters of the heart.
 He loves his wife, Penelope. He wasn't yours to
   take.

CALYPSO
 Not mine? Not mine? That's the richest yet.
 Who found him clinging to the keel of his boat
 at the height of the storm? Who plucked him
 out of the thrashing waves, kissed breath
 back into his lungs, pumped his heart with blood,
 nursed him back to strength, rolled him in love?
 Not mine? Without me there is no Odysseus.

HERMES
 You saved him from death. Does that mean he owes
   you his life?

CALYPSO
 I saved him from Poseidon, who clicked his fingers
 and smashed his boat to splinters
 and turned the ocean bed into a mass grave.
 While Zeus looked the other way, no doubt.

HERMES
 You should speak more quietly.

[38]

This cave amplifies an angry voice,
throws sounds upwards into the skies.

CALYPSO
Let it ring loud in the spirals of Zeus' ear.
If it's decided, what difference can it make?

HERMES
You can't win –
why make it more difficult for yourself?
Besides which, his actions aren't yours to judge.
Be glad you don't carry the burden of the world.

Don't light a fuse under the temper of mighty Zeus.

CALYPSO
This is a water-locked land, with no ships at anchor.

HERMES
You'll think of something. Use your ingenuity.

CALYPSO
Do you think I can just whistle and the navy appears?

HERMES
You saved him once, you can save him again.

CALYPSO
Well, if he drowns, don't lay the blame at my feet.
I don't want disfiguring with a thunderbolt.

HERMES
If you care for Odysseus as you say you do
you'll see him safe and sound out of the bay.
And if he's as keen to see his homeland as I think he is,
he'll take care of himself after that.

Will you give Odysseus the news, or shall I?

CALYPSO

You fly off home, errand boy.
I'll say my own goodbye.

ODYSSEUS ON THE ROCK

Calypso finds Odysseus looking out to sea. He is weeping.

CALYPSO
Tearful Odysseus. You could have been my God.

ODYSSEUS
Tears are human. They make me a man.

CALYPSO
You've wept an ocean from those eyes.

ODYSSEUS
If I had, I'd plunge into it here and now
and swim for home, buoyed up by the salt.
But this island sucks up everything I am.

CALYPSO
I am to give you up, Odysseus.

ODYSSEUS
You've tormented me too long for your jibes to hurt.

CALYPSO
But have I ever told you lies? Look into my face.

ODYSSEUS
It's a trick.

CALYPSO
Look into my eyes. Listen to my voice.
You're free to leave. I'm to give you up.

ODYSSEUS
Give me up? Give me up to what? Feed me to the sharks,
do you mean?

Put me to sea on a log so the waves can snap my bones?
Is that how you spit me out
after chewing the best years out of my life?

CALYPSO

The sharks aren't my pets. I don't control the waves.
But I'll help you leave by whatever means I possess.

ODYSSEUS

Why? I need to know why.

CALYPSO

Be happy to be heading home and don't ask.
Fate has decided, and no one can contradict fate.

ODYSSEUS

Fate lies in the flick of your wrist. You're a Goddess.

CALYPSO

Then don't dare interrogate me – treat me with respect.
Think of it, a Goddess indeed, who offered herself
to a mere man. But that man pines for his earthly wife.
By day you weep. At night, I pull you onto my body
and you only half-resist, but your thoughts are elsewhere
and you close your eyes to see Penelope's face.
So ask me nothing else. I might not have the human touch
you seem to crave, Odysseus, but I have my pride.
You should be grateful before I change my mind.

ODYSSEUS

It's true then? I'm free to go?
(*flattering her, not wanting to lose his chance*)
Calypso, have I ever once compared you to her?
My wife's face fades in my memory each day,
and that's what I can't bear. That's why I ache.
But your beauty will never dim because you never age.

CALYPSO

Your tongue was always your sharpest weapon.

ODYSSEUS

But it never cut you, no matter how close you came.

CALYPSO

Take this axe. Choose the sturdiest trees
for a raft, and build a hold on the deck.
I'll stow it with water and food
and wine to ease the passing of days.
I'll stitch warm clothes onto your back
and hang a full white sail from the mast.

ODYSSEUS

Can all this be true? Are the Gods smiling on me at last?

CALYPSO

I'm giving you my word. Here, give me your hand.

Lie with me one more night and leave at dawn.
Feel for yourself the compassionate heart in my breast.

THE PALACE OF ODYSSEUS

The suitors are dining.

EURYMACHUS
Bring me some horse.

AMPHINOMUS
You're drunk. We don't eat horse. Do we?

EURYMACHUS
I'll eat anything when I'm hungry.

ANTINOUS
You'll eat anything even when you're not.

EURYMACHUS
The stomach expects it.
Have you ever seen the inside of a man?

AMPHINOMUS
In battle, there was a wounded . . .

EURYMACHUS
I once tied a dead man's gut to a post
and fastened the other end to a messenger boy
and sent him off.
He walked for more than a mile and it still didn't snap.
It's elastic!
There's no limit to what you can trough,
and once you've stretched your appetite like that,
it's no good just eating a light snack.
Your stomach demands more.
(*shouts*)
Bring me some horse!

ANTINOUS
    We should have tied such a gut
    to Odysseus' son. Kept a hold on him.

EURYMACHUS
    It was your idea to let him go.

ANTINOUS
    So it was. But now I'm troubled by second thoughts.

AMPHINOMUS
    You said he was only a boy. You said he'd drown.

ANTINOUS
    I did.
    Then I heard he'd taken the swiftest boat
    in the land, and a careful choice of supplies,
    and hand-picked the best crew in town.
    And something else.

EURYMACHUS
    What?

ANTINOUS
    He was seen on the beach that night, in deep talk
    with that shady visitor – remember the one?

AMPHINOMUS
    The friend of his father's?
    Who disappeared as mysteriously as he came?

ANTINOUS
    That's what I was told.

AMPHINOMUS
    Maybe the old man was right, about those eagles
    grappling in mid-air. I found a feather
    in the courtyard that night, right under my foot . . .

EURYMACHUS

So what? I found a beetle in my shoe. So what?

ANTINOUS

Exactly. So what? On the other hand . . .

AMPHINOMUS

On the other hand . . .?

ANTINOUS

We should put to sea.

AMPHINOMUS

He'll be out of reach by now.
We'll never catch him up.

ANTINOUS

Not catch him up. More subtle than that.
We should lie in wait.

EURYMACHUS

I like the sound of this. Go on.

ANTINOUS

On his return leg,
Telemachus will sail that strait of water
between the cliffs of Samos and Ithaca's coast.
He might be planning a surprise for us,
but we'll have a bigger surprise for him.

EURYMACHUS

Yes, yes.

ANTINOUS

We'll flag him down, like a welcome party
meaning to sail with him into his home port.

EURYMACHUS
    That's crafty. Very crafty.

ANTINOUS
    We'll come alongside . . . and the rest
    we can leave to our imaginations, for now.
    Except to say
    he won't put so much as his little toe on home soil again.
        Agreed?

EURYMACHUS
    Agreed.

AMPHINOMUS
    You're talking about murder. Murdering the son
    of the woman you hope to marry.

ANTINOUS
    She'll marry no one if he comes sailing home from sunny
        Pylos
    bronzed with his father's reputation, swaggering and
        walking tall.
    Besides, she'll think he drowned by accident.
    Then she'll need a shoulder to cry on.

    But keep it under your tongues,
    we don't want loose talk whispering through the vaults
    or echoing into the upstairs chambers.

Their mumbling voices carry into the corridors of the house.

PENELOPE'S BED-CHAMBER

There is a tap at the door.

EURYCLEIA
  My lady?

PENELOPE
  Eurycleia?

EURYCLEIA
  Yes. Me, my lady.

PENELOPE
  I didn't call for you. It's too early.

Eurycleia taps at the door again.

EURYCLEIA
  My lady. My lady.

PENELOPE (*to herself*)
  Time has stuck its fingers
  in the old nurse's ears.
  I said you're excused.
  At least don't stand pawing at the door like a stray dog.
  Haven't we known each other long enough to . . .
  (*She opens the door.*)
  Eurycleia?

EURYCLEIA
  My lady. Forgive me.

PENELOPE
  Forgive you for what?
  Are the suitors skriking for more food?

[48]

Are they screaming like baby birds,
can't we feed them quick enough?
Well, open the doors of the granary
and the vaults where the meats are kept cold.
Let them gorge till they burst.

EURYCLEIA
If only they'd stuffed themselves silly,
then maybe I wouldn't be standing here like this.

PENELOPE
Standing like what?

EURYCLEIA
Like the thing that I am.
A raggedy old woman with bad news.

PENELOPE
What bad news?

EURYCLEIA
Don't hate me for it . . .

PENELOPE
Spit it out.

EURYCLEIA
It's Telemachus. He's gone.

PENELOPE
Gone where?

EURYCLEIA
Sailed off in search of his father. He was overheard on the
beach, making plans. And seen at the front of a ship as
it left the bay.

PENELOPE
Without telling me? Without saying . . .

EURYCLEIA
And there's worse, my lady. Oh, don't be hating me for
this.

PENELOPE
Say all of it. Tell it in one piece.

EURYCLEIA
Those slavering letches downstairs. Those drooling
mongrels not fit to kiss the soles of your shoes. They're
planning . . .

PENELOPE
All of it.

EURYCLEIA
. . . planning his death.
They'll lie in wait between the rocks. Cut him off on his
way back. Meet his body with bronze spears. They say
he'll never set foot on his homeland again. Oh my
lady . . .

PENELOPE
So either way he's lost. Sucked down by the sea
on his journey out, or slaughtered by cowards
within touching distance of his own shore, in front of his
mother's eyes.
First my husband was blown out of reach.
Now the wind carries my son off like a weightless seed.

Why wasn't I told?

EURYCLEIA
We were feared. There was only me daft enough.

Only me with a tongue that wasn't tied.
And anyway, he made me swear an oath.

PENELOPE
What oath?

EURYCLEIA
To say nothing – that's what I had to swear. So I was
torn down the middle, either to his loyalty, or to
yours. And he looked at me with a face like metal and
made me swear. Didn't want your beautiful skin
staining with tears – that's what he said. But if I did
wrong, then have me killed, my lady, and I'll not
complain. If I made the wrong choice, I'll hang up this
life on its peg. Like an old coat. Then you'll not be
nuisanced by me again.

PENELOPE
You were given no choice.
There will be no more talk of death.

EURYCLEIA
My lady.

PENELOPE
No more talk of loss.
(*She sways.*)
See how heavy my heart has swollen,
it pitches within me and bundles me over.
Steady me with your hand.

EURYCLEIA (*relieved, and full of love*)
Here's my hand, my lady, and your lovely hand in it.
Take strong hold of me. Let's wash with water, and I'll
find fresh clothes from the laundry. We'll go to the
upper house and pray to Athena.

PENELOPE (*tearful*)
  My only son.

EURYCLEIA
  And Odysseus' son – there'll be Gods watching over him,
  you can bet on that. This family hasn't fought its last
  fight, not by a long measure. Come, my lady.

OLYMPUS

Athena is looking down towards earth.

ZEUS

Athena, what are you gazing at now, or need I ask?

ATHENA

Look, father. Our messenger did his work.
Calypso releases Odysseus from her keep.

ZEUS

I find it doesn't do to look down too much like that.
Gives one a bad neck.

ATHENA

Zeus prefers to turn a blind eye. Is that it?

ZEUS

Zeus prefers a quiet life.

ATHENA

See how she dresses him in scented clothes for the trip.

ZEUS

I waste my breath.

ATHENA

And stows drink on his raft in animal skins.
One of pure water straight from the mountain spring.
One of heavy wine so he might sleep and dream.

ZEUS

If he sleeps he should tie himself to the mast.
There's trouble brewing.

ATHENA
  And gives him a sack full of food. And kisses him.

ZEUS
  It's of no interest to me.

ATHENA
  And he kisses her back.

ZEUS
  Really? So he does.

ATHENA
  Then she lets him go. Lets go of his arms, his fingers, his
    fingertips . . .

ZEUS
  Watches him out of sight. Will he turn and wave?

ATHENA
  It seems not.

ZEUS
  No, the sail stiffens into shape.
  He digs at the water with his oar,
  and keeps the rudder tight.

  Past the headland
  and the jagged rocks to the west, and over the reef.

  An open sea. And an open sky for the minute.
  He'll be clocking the stars tonight, charting the earth by
    the heavens,
  watching the moon's curve.
  Heading for home.

ATHENA

    Except, being mighty Zeus,
    it wouldn't do to watch. Right?

ZEUS

    Exactly so. Or at least
    we should save our viewing for when the action really
       starts.

ATHENA

    What do you mean by that?

ZEUS

    There's a rough ride ahead.

ATHENA

    A killer whale?

ZEUS

    Poseidon.

ATHENA

    That's who I meant.

ZEUS

    Poseidon indeed.
    Look at the twitching surface of the sea.
    My brother stirs in the deep.
    Brooding. Biding his time.

    All the signs are there.

ODYSSEUS ON HIS RAFT

ODYSSEUS
Seventeen days is it now?
Or eighteen. I lose count.
I should have notched the mast
every time it fell dark
or at every dawn.
But I've no knife or blade.
Only these fingernails,
broken and black.
Still, I'll cling to these timbers.

Holding this crude rudder tight
and using heaven's glittering chart
I've sailed in a straight line.
I'm weary, and my mind drifts,
but one thought – the thought of
home – keeps my hopes high.
Keeps me afloat. Landfall. Penelope.

Although, off to the west, the waves
seem to gallop and buck.
Don't say they're stampeding this way.
I'll hunker down, pray that they pass.

*

An hour later. The storm rages.

ODYSSEUS (*defiant, shouting to heaven*)
Is this death, then? Is it? IS THIS DEATH?
What a dirty trick. What a pitiful, pathetic,

miserable, side-winding death this is for me,
Odysseus, the unkillable genius hero of Troy,
with a hundred spears aimed at his chest
and a thousand arrows bouncing off his helmet and
    breast.
Now THAT WOULD HAVE BEEN GLORIOUS
    DEATH.
But no, it follows him over the waves, waits
till he's half-alive without armour or weapons
and crashes the whole sea onto his head.
Well, bring on the murderer. Bring on death.
Here I am. Here's a feather for your cap.
Shall I wave my arms about? Do you see me?
Let it be no secret, how miserable death
needed the force of Poseidon to kill one man.
Come ON. GIVE ME EVERYTHING YOU'VE GOT.

*A huge wave breaks over the raft. The mast splits. Odysseus
is thrown screaming into the ocean.*

OLYMPUS

Zeus and Athena follow Odysseus' progress.

ZEUS

He's a feisty one.

ATHENA

That's enough now. Call Poseidon off. Do SOMETHING.

ZEUS

No need. Look, the old sea-stirrer has turned tail.
He's had his say, made his feelings known.

ATHENA

And left Odysseus for dead.

ZEUS

No, not dead. Well, not yet, anyway.
Look, he clings to a plank of wood.

ATHENA

And what chance has he, cast adrift like that?

ZEUS

Slim. I wouldn't trade places with him, that's for sure.

But now that man and God have locked horns
and gone their separate ways,
maybe it wouldn't do any harm to er . . . how shall we
    say . . .
soothe the winds, usher them back to their quarters.

Or tug at Odysseus with a gentle hand,
steer him towards land for two or three days,
keep the sharks busy with some other scent.

[58]

The island of the Phaeacians lies ahead.
The rocks there are barbarous. Like metal teeth,
not just above the waves but underneath,
so a little swell of the sea wouldn't go amiss,
some little upsurge at the right moment in time
to land him safe on dry land. He'll be cold,
of course, and soaked to the bone, and dazed.
He'll need a path to open up through the woods,
and a place to bed down, between two olive trees
grown from the same root, for instance,
and a hugging of dry, dead leaves for a blanket.
He might sleep then, like a grain of fire
buried underground, where it can glow,
a secret spark, unnoticed, but ready to flare up.
Something of that sort wouldn't be out of turn,
if you were minded that way. Athena? Athena?

But Athena has already left.

She never did need telling twice, that one.
(*musing to himself*)
Excellent bedding, dead leaves. Dry for one thing.
Soft. Warm. Not too heavy. Make a good nest.
That's how I'd choose to hole up if it were me.

PHAEACIA

The rustle of dead leaves. Odysseus emerges from his nest.

ODYSSEUS (*jumping from his sleep, then muttering*)
    What? Where have I crash-landed now?
    What nowhere is this? What empty land
    am I dumped on this time, like the sea's litter?

    You Gods, did you give me a heart like a lemon,
    the rind too thick to take on water,
    bobbing endlessly from island to island?

    What am I in your eyes – just sea-junk,
    slewing from shore to shore with flotsam and driftwood?

    (*He hears a noise.*)
    What people live here? Savages. Cannibals.
    Or not people at all but wild monsters.
    A land of claws and fangs.
    No doubt I'm already the scent of food
    in the nostrils of some beast of hell,
    already a taste on some rough animal's tongue.

    (*He hears Nausicaa singing as she washes her clothes in
      the stream.*)
    Or by some miracle of fortune
    an altogether gentler creature.

    (*He approaches her, clearing his throat.*)
    Don't jump or run away, lady.
    Don't be appalled by me.

NAUSICAA (*shocked, but standing her ground*)
A thing-person, made of mud and sticks. And it speaks.

ODYSSEUS
The storm made smithereens of my raft
and the current dragged me here.
I slept in a compost of insects and leaves.
I must look like living filth in your eyes.

NAUSICAA
Like someone who crawled from a grave.

ODYSSEUS
My own, if Poseidon had his way.

NAUSICAA
You have worms in your hair.

ODYSSEUS
The sea rolled me in its jaws for twenty days . . .

NAUSICAA
You have beetles between your toes.

ODYSSEUS
. . . then spat me out. Here's where I crawled.

NAUSICAA
Naked, except for soil, although as luck would have it
you wear a sprig of leaves where men must wear clothes.

ODYSSEUS
I . . . apologize.
Especially to her whose arms
spill like milk from her shoulders.
Is it a goddess or woman I beg kindness from?

NAUSICAA

I'm Nausicaa, daughter of Alcinous and Arete,
King and Queen of the Phaeacians.

ODYSSEUS

I throw myself on your mercy.

NAUSICAA

Most visitors to our island come laden with gifts.

ODYSSEUS

I own nothing except the tongue in my head.

NAUSICAA

Most choose to approach via the harbour.

ODYSSEUS

The four winds plotted my course. I had nothing
but two arms for oars and two feet for a rudder.
(*laying on the charm*)
Would any visitor dare come with such a reckless story
and wild manner, unless his circumstances were true?
Have me arrested and thrown in chains if you wish,
but . . . if there's some glimmer of light,
if you can see the man under this muddy suit . . .

I could follow you to the palace, but lag behind,
put some time and distance between your graceful
    footsteps
and my own. It wouldn't be right for a princess
to have her brightness diminished by such a dark sight.

NAUSICAA

Very well.
But first bathe in the water, and rub yourself in oil.
And here, wear this garment I brought to wash in the
    stream.

I'll . . . look away while you dress. Then I'll walk
with damp footsteps towards home,
and you'll follow before they fade in the heat.

She giggles and leaves.

ODYSSEUS (*whispering to himself*)
Oh Athena, Goddess obscured by the sky,
if you were deaf to me while the ocean
pulverized my bones, now hear my prayer.
Let me find some courtesy among these folk,
let them show compassion to this lost soul,
let them show mercy, even love.

Let them build me a boat.

AT THE PALACE OF THE PHAEACIANS

A supper is taking place.

ALCINOUS
  And you found him hiding in a pit, is that right?

NAUSICAA
  In a nest of leaves where he'd curled up for the night.

ARETE
  Was he fashionably dressed? Was he suitably attired?

NAUSICAA
  No, mother, he was nude.

ARETE
  He was what?

NAUSICAA
  Stark naked, except for leaves that had stuck with sweat,
  and insects and bugs that crawled in his tangled hair,
  and berries that had burst their redness against his
    skin . . .

ALCINOUS
  We see the image clearly, thank you, daughter.

ARETE
  A bog man wearing nothing but weeds.
  And you invited him here?

NAUSICAA
  I took pity. I gave him a cloak.

ARETE
He's come to murder us in our beds.

NAUSICAA
And oil to soothe his tired and aching limbs.

ARETE
Tell her, Alcinous. Tell your daughter
he means to put a knife in our ribs.
A stranger, come to trick his way into our house,
and she gives him the key.

ALCINOUS
Sounds like you acted in haste, Nausicaa.

NAUSICAA
I followed my instincts, just as I was taught.

ALCINOUS
Your instincts? Are you sure it wasn't your heart?

NAUSICAA
There's something about this man, father,
something more than meets the eye,
something elemental, naked, raw . . .

ARETE
I think we've already established that.

NAUSICAA
Well, see for yourself.

*A whispering silence descends as Odysseus enters the hall
and approaches the top table.*

ODYSSEUS
Your royal highnesses. Merciful princess.

ALCINOUS (*clearing his throat*)
We . . . er . . .
We expected some kind of walking, talking shrub.
A raspberry patch with arms and legs.
But from our first report you've undergone a change.
Speak up, stranger.

ODYSSEUS
Your daughter found me in a filthy, rotten heap
but gave me these robes, and oil for my wounds,
and more oils to bring the shine back to my skin.
The lamp of charity burns brightly in her heart.

ARETE
We won't be hoodwinked by flattery.

NAUSICA
Mother, give him a chance.

ODYSSEUS
No, your mother is right.
Even in these borrowed clothes I do no justice to this
    noble house.

So I'll be as blunt as I dare.
I'll be as crude as I am bare
under this ill-fitting gown.
I'll be as truthful as flesh and bone,
which is all that I am now
and which is all that I own.

I am . . .
(*with great boldness and courage*)
I am Odysseus. I AM ODYSSEUS,
son of Laertes, known the world over
for cunning and guile and strength of mind.

Odysseus – a hero of Troy.
My fame is written in the heavens,
and my fate too,
and my wife is Penelope,
and my son is Telemachus,
and my home is Ithaca,
but somewhere in the clockwork of islands and time and
    Gods, I'm lost.

Nymphs have held me back.
Armies have held me back.
Witches have held me back.
Sea monsters have held me back.
The one-eyed mumbling Cyclops,
the mind-melting songs of the sirens,
the deep narcotic of the lotus flower,
the prophecies of the dead,
whirlpools, clashing rocks . . .

No man loves his country or his family
more than me – the heart is a magnet,
it spins, and finds its true north, and pulls.
It tugs. Even while I sleep it tugs and tugs,
so homesickness is a permanent hurt,
a soreness, a physical tenderness – a bruise.

But the heart isn't a boat.
This heart alone won't sail me home,
and somewhere in this mad, wild, hurling clockwork
of islands and time and Gods, I'm lost.

NAUSICAA
My feelings were right. This man is set apart.
Bring him a seat.
Sit him close to the hearth and the warmth.

ARETE

    I advise caution. This is all moving very fast.

ALCINOUS

    We don't welcome strangers into our midst casually,
    Odysseus, but your speech persuades me . . .

ARETE

    He should be telling all this to the magistrate.

ALCINOUS

    Finish your story.
    If it rings true we'll carry you home to your journey's end.

ODYSSEUS

    It would take an age to tell.

ALCINOUS

    Take all the time you need. We'll listen and wait.

    Put a drink in his hand. SILENCE IN THE ROOM.
    Let nobody break the long, winding thread of his
        thoughts.
    Now, cast backwards, Odysseus, to where that strand
        begins.

ODYSSEUS (*composing himself*)

    It begins in glory, then tells of all the pain
    and misery the Gods have dreamed up for me since.

    We sailed from Troy, victorious.
    Achaeans with no thoughts other than home:
    Ithaca – the outstretched arms
    of its bay – our families – their love.
    The wind pushed us to Ismarus,
    land of the Cicones.
    We plundered the city, took meat

and wine and women and grain
to be shared equally among the men.
Then I ordered the retreat:
'Leave the rest. Back to the boats, everyone. Back to the
    coast.'

But my army was boggle-eyed
with treats, went on slaughtering
the plentiful flocks and herds,
and while they butchered and ate
and slept, the enemy grew,
drew strength from further afield,
gathered all night in the dark
then attacked out of the dawn mist,
cut us down like stalks,
flattened us into the battlefields.
Six men from every crew were lost,
the rest of us skedaddled in the boats.
Sick with grief, we saluted our dead,
then swung our oars into the water
and rowed and rowed and rowed . . .

II

ODYSSEUS AND HIS ARMY AT SEA

EURYLOCHUS
  You sent for me.

ODYSSEUS
  Any signs of landfall? Any omens?

EURYLOCHUS
  No nesting birds to speak of,
  but plenty of leaves in the sea, and a morning haze,
  and two river-dolphins yesterday. We must be close.

ODYSSEUS
  Nine days now.

EURYLOCHUS
  Nine not counting today.

ODYSSEUS
  How are the supplies?

EURYLOCHUS
  Some boats low on water on account of what was spilt
  when we pushed off in all that mayhem.
  Some boats low on food.

ODYSSEUS
  And the men?

EURYLOCHUS
  Grumbling like dogs. Nothing new in that.
  Want to find land soon so they can light a fire – cook up a
      hot meal.
  They say they're sick of pecking at raw flesh.
  They say they're not crows.

ODYSSEUS
No more dead?

EURYLOCHUS
No more. The Cicones weren't aiming to wound. They
knew how to kill.

ODYSSEUS
We brought it on ourselves, Eurylochus.
We should have taken what we needed and no more.
Instead of gorging on mutton and beef.
We got what we deserved. We were animals.

EURYLOCHUS
When you've been away from home so long,
when you've prowled from one skirmish to the next,
when you stink of the world – that's how it feels.
These men need to get home. They're turning wild.

SAILOR (*off*)
LAND.

ODYSSEUS
Who calls out?

EURYLOCHUS
The front boat, away in the mist.
(*to the front boat*)
Shout again.

SAILOR (*off*)
Land ahead, and a harbour, and sand to beach in.

ODYSSEUS (*shouting to the other boats*)
Follow their wake. Follow their wake.
(*to Eurylochus*)
We'll take on water,

[74]

make a fire for the night, give sacrifice and prayer,
roast the best of the meat.
And send a party of three men inland –
see what people live there – people like us, perhaps –
and if there are breads or crops to be had.
Then we'll sail first thing next day.

EURYLOCHUS (*repeating the order*)
Follow their wake.

THE LOTUS EATERS

*Next morning, on the coast of a tropical paradise, with
exotic birds calling from the interior and waves washing
gently against the shore.*

ODYSSEUS
A bright morning, a waiting sea and a friendly wind. All
prepared?

EURYLOCHUS
All the pots and bags filled and all stowed.

ODYSSEUS
And all the men counted and numbered?

EURYLOCHUS
Except for the three you sent inland.

ODYSSEUS
What time did they set out?

EURYLOCHUS
Just before dusk last night.

ODYSSEUS
And no sign of them since?

EURYLOCHUS
Not a sniff.

ODYSSEUS
Which way did they go?

EURYLOCHUS
That steep path by the cliff. See, where those flowers
bloom.

ODYSSEUS
You mean the . . . which flowers? Not those?

EURYLOCHUS
Beautiful, aren't they? And the smell.
I'd swear the scent of them was making me quite light-
  headed last night.
I dreamed of when I was a boy, in my father's garden . . .

ELPENOS (*calls out*)
My beautiful leader. My beautiful friends.

EURYLOCHUS
Here they are. Call off the search party.

ODYSSEUS
Bring me a rope from the ship.

EURYLOCHUS
I thought you wanted to sail. Now you want to hunt?

EURYBATES
Come here by the flowers. Come and feast with us.

ANTIPHUS
Odysseus, bliss to you, my king, bliss, my friend.

EURYLOCHUS
Are they drunk? Have they found wine?

ODYSSEUS
Not wine, something far more potent.
Those are lotus flowers. The fruit and the seed
when taken on the tongue . . . they say
the gates of perception are flung wide and the spirit soars.
But when the feeling dies, the soul enters a chasm.

Worse than that – if the lotus gets into our blood
we'll lose all judgement and sense;

we need minds quicker than knives and sharper than
    swords
or we'll never reach home. Fetch the rope.

The three scouts approach Odysseus.

ELPENOS
    Odysseus, come taste what we've found.
    Honey of all honey. Sugar of all sweetness.

ANTIPHUS
    My king, you have landed us in paradise.

EURYBATES
    Such smoothness enters the mind.
    Colours are endless and limitless.

ANTIPHUS
    Ask me what I feel, my beautiful comrade.
    I feel a vast, velvet pleasantness.

EURYBATES
    I feel purple ecstasy.

ANTIPHUS
    I feel harmony. The golden harmony.

ODYSSEUS
    Take nothing from them. Don't even smell their breath.

ELPENOS
    The rapture of all mankind uncurls in me.
    The Gods are in my bloodstream.
    All the joy of existence, the rush of life . . .

EURYBATES
    And the wonder, the wonder, the wonder . . .
    Every nerve in my body vibrates in orgasm . . .

ODYSSEUS

Rope these three and haul them back to the ship.

ELPENOS

Ropes. Not ropes. Why ropes, Odysseus?

ODYSSEUS

And search their pockets for those fatal plants.

ANTIPHUS (*beginning to panic*)

Odysseus, comrade, beautiful friend, don't pain me.
It's all here and it's all free.

ODYSSEUS

Be quiet. Pull yourself together.

ANTIPHUS

Taste it for yourself – the essence of it.
Don't pain me, Odysseus? Odysseus?
Give me my flower.
GIVE ME MY FLOWER.

ELPENOS (*weeping like a child*)

It isn't yours to take away.
You've got your own Gods, why can't we worship the
    flower,
float in the fever of its pollen for ever?

ODYSSEUS

Give me that stuff. Throw it on the floor. All of it.

ANTIPHUS (*sobbing*)

You destroyers, you killjoys, you assassins, you
    executioners . . .
This is rape. This is THE MURDER OF LOVE.
This isn't FAIR.

EURYBATES
  Get these ropes off. NOW.
  YOU BASTARDS.

ODYSSEUS
  Turn out his pockets.

EURYBATES
  Leave my pockets alone.
  Those flowers are mine, mine,
  mine, mine, mine, mine, mine (*dissolves in tears*)

The three men are hauled back to the ship protesting and
weeping pathetically.

ODYSSEUS (*shouting after them*)
  Tie them on deck until they stop jabbering.
  And wash your hands in the sea. I want no pollen
  of that crazy species dusting the air
  or spiking the wine or seasoning the food,
  or taking root under someone's boot.
  I won't carry it home.

  Scrub them of every spore.

IN THE PALACE OF THE PHAEACIANS

ODYSSEUS

The wind rose, hauling us forward.
The drugged men wailed,
shivered until their bones rattled.
They puked and went pale. Then sat and stared,
their eyes sinking into their heads
like jewels thrown overboard.
Landfall came quickly. Before we knew it
the boats had run aground on a shelf,
whispered to a halt in soft sand. Land,
but not home. We'd heard the folklore
of that place, rumours of a one-eyed freak
roaming the cliffs. Cyclops – Poseidon's weird son.
We should have steered clear, but the thought of food
and fresh milk took us straight to his cave.

CYCLOPS

ODYSSEUS
This way, but no sudden noises.
You, man, go through those rocks and peer in.

ELPENOS
Has he really only one eye?

EURYBATES
That's what they say. So why should we fear – he's already
half blind.
What do you say, Polites?

POLITES
One eye only, but it's as wide and as deep and as clear
as a barrel of rain. So he'll see us all right, if he's in range.

ELPENOS
If his eye's so big there can't be much room for his ears.

EURYBATES
So we can sneak up on him while he looks the other way,
and he won't hear a thing!

POLITES
There's room all right, because his head is as big as a
boulder.
Now pipe down, before we find out.

SHIPMATE (*from the mouth of the cave*)
It's all clear. Nobody home.

POLITES
Are you sure?

SHIPMATE

Cave's empty – apart from the smell.

But these buckets aren't, and neither are these stalls.

Come and feast your eyes on this lot.

They run over to the mouth of the cave. The bleating of lambs and kids can be heard.

EURYBATES

Cornucopia. There must be five dozen heads here.

ELPENOS

Lamb *and* goat. We'll stuff our faces tonight.

ANTIPHUS

And snouters. I can hear them hissing and spitting on the
    fire already.

EURYBATES

What's in the buckets?

ELPENOS

Milk, is it?

EURYBATES

More like cheese, or whey.

ELPENOS

Well, whey – hey! It's like he knew we were coming and
    laid on a feast.

Let's get everything back to the boats.

ODYSSEUS

No, we should wait.

ELPENOS

Wait for what, Odysseus? Sir?

ODYSSEUS
   He might make us welcome here. Give us this food as
      a gift.

EURYBATES
   He's a one-eyed monster who eats people alive.
   I'm not hanging around to sample his hospitality.

ANTIPHUS
   Me neither. Here, help me herd these sheep.

ODYSSEUS
   I SAID WE WILL WAIT.
   We're not savages. We're Achaeans of Ithaca.
   Men of our word.
   We're not rampaging from shore to shore
   without cause,
   we're making the long journey home
   after a just war.
   Get your minds above your bellies for a minute.
   Greed and gluttony
   lost us half our men against the Cicones.
   You, make a fire.
   You, take modest portions of cheese and milk
   into the cave.
   We'll wait for our host. Today we'll be civilized.

The men grumble but follow his instructions.

   Everyone into the cave.

                              *

*Later. Around a crackling fire, the men sit chatting in the
echoing cave, waiting the return of Cyclops.*

ELPENOS
    What about you?

EURYBATES
    What about me?

ELPENOS
    What's the first thing you'll do when you get home?

EURYBATES
    Obvious, isn't it?

The rest of the men laugh and whistle.

ELPENOS
    All right, what's the second thing?

EURYBATES
    I'll probably do it again.

More laughter and whistling.

ANTIPHUS
    Tell you what I'll do. I've got a little plot of land above
    the cliff. It's not much but it feeds me and the family.
    It's probably gone to seed by now. Well, first I'll build
    the walls back up, make it all trim and tidy. Then I'll
    put a crop in the soil . . . barley or wheat. Then at dusk,
    I'll say a prayer to Zeus, and throw a stone in the sea,
    and swear on that stone never, ever, ever to set foot on
    a boat again. I'm going to plant myself in that field, and
    I'm going to take root.

ELPENOS
    I'll drink to that.

EURYBATES (*proposing a toast*)
    To Ithaca!

ALL
  To Ithaca!

ANTIPHUS
  Then I'll get off home to the wife for a bit of what you
    were talking about.

They all roar with laughter.

SHIPMATE
  Something approaches.

ODYSSEUS
  Is it him?

SHIPMATE
  He's . . . he's enormous.

ODYSSEUS
  Everyone right to the back of the cave,
  and total silence.

SHIPMATE
  He's enormous. Enormous!

ODYSSEUS
  Hold on to your thoughts, watchman,
  or I'll put my fist through your skull and hold them for
    you.
  Now quiet everyone.

*The Cyclops arrives at the mouth of the cave, grunting and
snuffling. He babbles and mutters to himself, then snooks,
clears his throat and spits out a ball of snot.*

ANTIPHUS (*whispering*)
  In heaven's name – he's inhuman.

EURYBATES

Look at those hands. He'll mangle us.

ELPENOS

We're done for, we're pulp.

SHIPMATE

I told you. He's enormous.

ODYSSEUS

Shut it. All of you, before he hears us.

CYCLOPS

Yahn,

Tayhn,

Tether,

Mether,

Mimph,

Hither,

Lither,

Danver,

Dic . . .

EURYBATES

What's he doing? What's he saying?

ODYSSEUS

He's counting his flock into the pen.

EURYBATES

What language is he speaking?

CYCLOPS

Yahndic,

Tayhndic,

Tetherdic,

Metherdic,

Mimphit,
Yahn-a-mimphit,
Tayhn-a-mimphit,
Tether-a-mimphit,
Mether-a-mimphit . . .

ANTIPHUS
It's baby-talk if you ask me. Gobbledygook language.

CYCLOPS (*hearing them*)
WHAT? Grokells! Infesters!
Who squatting in Cyclops' cave?
Who dodging and skulking in shadows in Cyclops' cave?

ODYSSEUS (*speaking up from the back*)
Pardon us.
We're men of Ithaca, blown off course
by cruel winds, at the mercy of the sea.
We fetched up here by chance. We mean
no harm and hope you might welcome us
as strangers in a strange land. We offer
the hand of friendship and our word.
We are true men, respecters of the Gods.

CYCLOPS
Gods!
(*He bellows with laughter.*)
Cyclops farts in Gods' faces. Cyclops pisses on Gods' feet.
Cyclops does whatever Cyclops please.
(*in a clumsy attempt at cunning*)
So, er, where did Ithaca men land them ship?

POLITES (*whispering*)
Don't tell him. He'll find it and crush it.

EURYLOCHUS
    Odysseus, throw him off the scent.

ODYSSEUS
    Our ship was wrecked.
    We entered the bay.
    We swam for our lives.
    Myself and the men that you see
    are all that's left.

*Cyclops mumbles and muses to himself, then giggles, then
mumbles and giggles some more.*

CYCLOPS
    Cyclops lonely. Cyclops on his own.

ELPENOS
    Aw, look at him, he's just a big kid.

EURYBATES
    He's grinning. You're right. He's a big soft lump really.

Cyclops giggles and laughs. The men begin to laugh.

ANTIPHUS
    He likes us. He thinks we're his friends – big dumb
        animal. Come on, let's help ourselves to this fodder.

ODYSSEUS
    Wait a second, let me talk to him some more.

ANTIPHUS
    It's fine. Hey, one-eye, how about me and you get our
        teeth stuck into that slab of cheese over there? I'll have
        the first bite . . .

Cyclops grabs the man and devours him. The other men scream and shout as Antiphus is crushed and eaten. Cyclops slabbers and drools and burps as he gobbles his victim, crunching his bones between his teeth.

ODYSSEUS
Everyone, get right back into the crag where he can't
  reach us.

POLITES
He's closing the door – we're trapped.

ELPENOS
We should have cut and run while we had the chance.
Now he's going to eat us alive one by one.

ODYSSEUS
Get right into the crack there.
Pack down, make room for everyone.

ELPENOS
He'll pluck us out with those long, gangling arms.
Where is he now?

POLITES
Pacing around the cave, looking this way.

CYCLOPS
GRRRRRNNNNNNNNAAAWWWWWW.

ELPENOS
He's got us right where he wants us.
We're dead meat. He'll just reach in and grab us.

ODYSSEUS
This fissure's too narrow for him
and we'll guard the entrance with spears.
We'll wait in this bolt-hole until morning.

ELPENOS

Why, so he can eat us for breakfast?

ODYSSEUS

Settle down and rest. We're safe here.
Be quiet and let me think.

CYCLOPS

GGGRRRRNNNNAAAWWWWWWWW.

Out of breath, the men cower at the back of the cave.

EURYBATES

Poor old Antiphus.
I don't suppose he'll be needing that field of his any more.

*

Morning in the cave. Cyclops is snoring. Sheep are bleating.

EURYBATES

My arm's gone to sleep.

ELPENOS

Move your leg. Your foot's right in my face.

ODYSSEUS

Watchman, can you see anything?

SHIPMATE

He's still asleep. He's got blood on his chin and bones
stuck in his teeth.

EURYLOCHUS

A hundred of us couldn't move that boulder from the
entrance.
He's bunged the hole. We're trapped like flies in a bottle.

ODYSSEUS
    All right, listen to me.
    Who has wine left in their sacks?
    Pour it all into this one bag.
    Let's see if Cyclops here can handle his drink.

ELPENOS
    He's already scoffed poor Antiphus. Now you're giving
        him wine to whet his appetite for the rest of us.

EURYBATES
    We should drink it ourselves – at least we'd die happy.

ODYSSEUS
    Hand it to Polites and Eurylochus.
    Trust me, this is our only means of escape.

*Odysseus emerges from the back of the cave and approaches
the stirring Cyclops.*

ODYSSEUS
    Wake up. Here's a peace offering from the men of Ithaca.

Cyclops grumbles.

ODYSSEUS
    Good wine, strong wine.
    It tastes better than men's blood.
    Drink this instead, and let us go. Here, catch.

He throws Cyclops the wine sack.

CYCLOPS
    What Ithaca man name?

ODYSSEUS
    My name? You want my name?
    Nobody, that's what they call me.

Nobody's my name.

CYCLOPS

Nobody? Huh, Nobody. Cyclops drink wine. Cyclops eat
Nobody last. Cyclops save Nobody for pudding. Ha!

*He laughs and begins guzzling the wine. Odysseus returns to
his men.*

ELPENOS

Well, that was a fat lot of good. Now he's got the wine
and us. If Odysseus ever goes into the bartering
business he'll be bankrupt in a week.

Cyclops starts gurgling and singing to himself.

ODYSSEUS

Listen to him – he's a stranger to wine.
He doesn't know the boozy fumes of the grape.
Wait till it floods through his veins,
wait till it loosens the knot of his brain.

Cyclops burps and laughs and glugs more of the wine.

Eurylochus, Polites.
And you, man, and you, and you.
See that log in the ogre's fire – the longer one?
See its pointed end – it glows red with heat.
Come with me when I give the word, hoist it
onto my shoulder, then push from behind.
I'll aim it into the soul of that creature's life.

POLITES

Into his heart to kill him?

ODYSSEUS

No, comrades, into his eye.

We'll blind him, but we need him alive.

Cyclops is humming to himself and laughing.

Follow me.
Hush now. More stealth.
Softly – here by the fire.
That's the one.
See the tip – like a branding iron.
Lift it after three.
One . . . two . . . three.
(*straining under the weight*) Ngg . . .
Forward.
Steady it.
Hold it there.

Hey, Cyclops, over here. Are you awake? Are you open
  eyed?

CYCLOPS
Who shout Cyclops?
Nobody man. Cyclops hungry now for Nobody.

ODYSSEUS
Here I am, in the shadow.
(*to his men*)
Look how his pupil dilates. Wait till it stretches wide.
(*to Cyclops*)
See me now? Here by the rock. Here's Nobody for you.

CYCLOPS
GGGGGGGGRRRRRRRNNNAAWWWWWWW.

ODYSSEUS
Do you see me? Do you see Nobody?

ELPENOS

He'll smash us to pieces.

EURYBATES

The Gods have deserted us. He's got the jaw of a lion.

ELPENOS

And the teeth of a shark.

POLITES

This is doomed, Odysseus.

ODYSSEUS

Hold your position. Here he comes.

CYCLOPS

Cyclops eat now,
chew Nobody's flesh.
bite out Nobody's heart,
tear off Nobody's head. . . . GGNNNAWWWW.

ODYSSEUS

NOW!

*The men run forward and drive the burning stake into
Cyclops' eye. He lets out an ear-splitting scream. The stake
fizzes as his eye burns and boils.*

Drive. Drive. Drive.
Ram it all the way home . . .

CYCLOPS

NNNNNAAAAARRGGHHHHHHHH . . .

ODYSSEUS

Now twist and gouge,
now heave, heave, heave, heave . . .

IN THE PALACE OF THE PHAEACIANS

ODYSSEUS
    . . . heave, heave.
Then all the men came and added their weight,
hammered that burning stake into his head,
and when the eyeball burst we were soaked in ink,
and the lens crunched and cracked like splintering ice,
and the lashes and eyebrows flared like burning grass,
and we leaned, and heaved, and forced it further in
until the retina sheared, and the optic nerve
spat and seared and spasmed and fused in the heat.
All the while he screamed into the cave,
roared his pain into the booming, echoing rock,
so loud that other one-eyed monsters on the island
came to listen. They gathered outside, more curious
than concerned, and called, 'Hey, you in there,
what's all the fuss and palaver? Who's giving you grief?'
And Cyclops, writhing in pain, his head in flames,
shouted, 'Nobody. Nobody hurts Cyclops. Nobody.'

So they shrugged their shoulders and padded off home.
A master-stroke on my part, and it worked.
When we drew out the stake it was like a bung,
like a cork, like a plug – blood spurted and plumed,
but I didn't finish him off, the thick-headed brute. Why?
He'd rolled a stone across the cave's mouth, blocking the
      gap,
a stone so vast that he alone could shift it from the hole.
And this was the whole point of my ingenious plan.
The flock were cowering away from the noise and flames.
Twines and twisted willow-strands littered the floor.

Each man lashed himself tight under a fat ram,
and two other rams were tethered alongside
to shield him at the flanks as he dangled and clung on.
Then they ambled forward, tottered over the stone floor,
bleated to be let out of the cave for water and pasture,
and Cyclops, even with a smoking hole instead of an eye,
was still a shepherd at heart, so he rolled away the rock,
opened the mouth of the cave and counted them out,
stroking their backs as they wandered into the light:
'Mether, Tether, Mimph, Hither, Lither, Anver, Danver . . .'
The ignorant swine, he released them one at a time,
each big ram with one of my men slung under its gut.
And I was the last man to escape, suspended beneath
the cockiest ram of the lot, my fingers twisted
into the deep shag of his coat, my feet stirrupped
in the swags of elastic skin to the inside of his leg.

Once on the boats with the men and the flock
and the buckets of cheeses and barrels of milk,
I goaded the Cyclops with taunts, and he hurled rocks
from the cliff but they only caused ripples
that pushed us further to sea. The wide open sea.

And the men cheered and laughed until light . . .
when it dawned on us that nothing had changed.

Still lost, still famished-hearted, still years from home,
but now with Poseidon fuming and writhing below us,
plotting revenge for blinding his one-eyed son.

That act was to haunt us. From then on
we were marked men, locked on a collision course
with the God of the Sea. He lurked in the depths,
a constant presence. We sensed him under the waves.
The boat shivered when he stirred. And if we'd have known

the chain of events we'd set in place, the cruelty
and agony that stretched ahead, year after year,
the horror and terror and sadness and loss still to come –
   who knows,
perhaps we'd have chosen to die right there, in the black
   cave,
out of sight of heaven and without sound.

With our fate now in the hands of the Gods
we drifted on wind and current, hoping again,
hoping against hope, praying, looking for land.

IN THE PALACE OF THE PHAEACIANS

Stunned silence follows Odysseus' story.

ALCINOUS

Odysseus, yours is a fantastical tale . . .

NAUSICAA

Such adventure and excitement, and such bravery.
Hearing it causes a drum-roll in my heart.

ARETE

Breathtaking all right. Flabbergasting in fact.
Blinding the Cyclops with a burning branch,
then escaping tied to a ram – do we believe this man?

ODYSSEUS

Courteous King Alcinous, graceful Queen Arete,
Princess Nausicaa, who salvaged me in the woods,
and you Phaeacians, who tolerate my company,

what I've told you so far is only the start, fabulous
as it might seem. The mind-altering lotus plant,
the puddle-eyed Cyclops with his taste for flesh –
there's enough weirdness and terror right there
to fill a man's days, you might think, and you'd be right.
But they're nothing compared to what lay ahead.

Let me explain how outrageous twists of fortune and fate
led me to your island in this ruined state.

ALCINOUS

You have our permission and our attention.

NAUSICAA
  We're entranced, enraptured, aren't we, father?
  So, you blinded the Cyclops with a red-hot pile-driver,
  left him shaking his fist at the top of the cliff . . .

ODYSSEUS
  Seething, cursing, tearing up rocks and lumps of earth
  to hurl at the ship, calling his father, Poseidon, to rise
  from the deep and clatter us, feed us to the fish.

  But we rode out the storm, and landed by chance
  on the Island of Aeolia, home of good Aeolus,
  whose palace shines like a mirage above the sea,
  whose halls and rooms are thick – night and day –
  with the smell of freshly roasted beasts and fish and game.

  He hosted us royally. Not one of our needs went
      unattended,
  and before we sailed he gave me a cloth bag, tightly
      strung,
  with the south wind, the north, and the wind from the
      east
  bundled inside, so not one breath could blow us off
      course,
  but the west wind he kept free to puff us gently along.

  Yet his kindly thoughts were wasted on us.
  Nine days on, we gave in to our weaknesses and faults.

THE BAG OF WIND

SHIPMATE
Land. I see land.

ELPENOS
I see it too.

EURYBATES
Where?

ELPENOS
To the left. Look, can't you see the trees?

EURYBATES
No. Where? Yes, now I see it, through the mist.

ELPENOS
And fires. Men setting fires at dusk.

Wait a second, look at that promontory. Look, look.

EURYBATES
He's right – see the shape of the bay and the bluff. It can't
be. It can't be.

ELPENOS
Ithaca – oh, make a sacrifice to Zeus. We'll slaughter the
proudest animal on the island as soon as we set foot on
solid ground. We're home. WE'RE HOME!

There is jubilation amongst the men.

EURYLOCHUS
All eyes to the port side.
Praise be to mighty Zeus who returns us home.
Odysseus? Odysseus?

ODYSSEUS (*at the other end of the boat, to himself*)
    I see it, my men. I saw it an hour ago.
    Wouldn't allow myself to believe it.
    Willing it, trying to make it materialize.
    Stared so hard and long I'm hypnotized,
    dazed by it. Ithaca – I hardly dare say it
    in case it breaks like a dream and disappears.

    (*to the men*)
    An hour or so until we put in. Make ready.
    And scrub yourselves, and scour every deck.
    Shout the orders across the boats. Pride, men.
    We won't return like ragamuffins and louts.
    Stitch every tear. Cover your wounds.
    Comb the salt from your beards, and smile!
    We'll come home as handsome as we left,
    and with honour, and with Troy to our name.

EURYLOCHUS
    Odysseus, sir. Come and drink with the crew.

ODYSSEUS
    No, I won't. Suddenly I'm . . . overcome.
    As if every muscle and nerve
    has been stretched and strained for twenty years.
    Twenty years hardly daring to sleep or even blink.
    I feel . . . fantastically tired.

EURYLOCHUS
    But you can relax now, we're home.

ODYSSEUS
    I'll sleep for a while. Wake me as we land.

EURYLOCHUS
I will, I'll be ready with clean clothes and a meal.

*

Later, approaching the shore of Ithaca.

SHIPMATE
Is there a drink there for me?

ELPENOS
Help yourself.

SHIPMATE
I will indeed. Well, here's to home, and Odysseus.

EURYBATES
I'll drink to the first all right, but not the second.

SHIPMATE
You won't raise a toast to your captain and king,
who guided us back to our own coast,
saved us from certain death time and time again?

ELPENOS
It was luck. He's just a lucky son of a . . .

SHIPMATE
Watch your tongue or you'll be shark-meat, friend.

EURYBATES
Let him speak. Because he's right, isn't he? Look at him
    now, asleep on a plump cushion, adored the world over,
    worshipped like a God. And why – because fortune
    smiles on him – that's all. Not like me. If I fell in a
    barrel of bosoms I'd come out sucking my thumb. He's
    the golden one.

SHIPMATE
He's got foresight and acumen and charisma.

ELPENOS
That isn't all he's got.

SHIPMATE
Explain yourself.

ELPENOS
Booty. Plunder. The spoils of war – that's what I'm talking about.

EURYBATES
Exactly.

ELPENOS
All the swag that he's bringing home from Troy, while us lot who stood and scrapped on the front line come home penniless and broken.

SHIPMATE
It's nothing more than he's entitled to.
It's appropriate to his position.

ELPENOS
It's greed. Self-indulgence.

EURYBATES
Look what happened only nine days ago. Aeolus gives him a bag of goodies which he squirrels away. More riches for him and two fingers to the rest of us. Well, I won't stand for it any longer.

SHIPMATE
Don't do anything rash, not now. We'll soon be in port.

ELPENOS

Aye, soon be shambling down that gangplank like
paupers, while Odysseus saunters home with a king's
ransom. Fetch that bag!

SHIPMATE

This is very irregular.

EURYBATES

No, it's equality. Fairness. Where did he hide it?

ELPENOS

In that locker. No, the bottom one. Under the shelf.

SHIPMATE

I'll have to inform him – it's my duty.

ELPENOS

Go on then, go running to him. Or why not have a little
squint in this bag? See what you're missing. See if
there's anything you fancy.

SHIPMATE

No, I . . . Well, I . . .

ELPENOS

A little look won't harm, will it?

SHIPMATE (*gulps*)

Just a peep perhaps, no crime in that. Since you're
opening it anyway.

EURYBATES

Here we go. It's a bit light. No precious stones, that's for
sure.

ELPENOS

Pass it here. Whoa! It's squirming. Must be an animal.

Some rare species bred for its perfume – worth a
fortune, I bet. Whooaaa! Keep still, you crazy ferret.
Anyone got a knife?

SHIPMATE
Let me, let me! I mean, you can borrow mine if you want.

ELPENOS
Hold it straight while I slit the drawstring.
(*struggling with it*)
What is it tied with, wire? Ah, nearly there. One last . . .
GOT IT.

*There is a huge rush of air, building up and up, as if a
hurricane has been let loose on the ship. The winds of the
south, east and north whip themselves into a frenzy.*

ODYSSEUS (*running towards them*)
NO! CLOSE THE BAG. CLOSE THE BAG.

SHIPMATE
Odysseus. Help us.

ODYSSEUS
Who opened the bag? Who freed the winds?

SHIPMATE
The men – they wanted their fair share.

ODYSSEUS (*incredulous*)
Fair share of what?

SHIPMATE
Whatever it held. They wanted some for themselves.

ODYSSEUS (*full of bitterness and fury*)
Well, now they have it. Tell them to hold on for dear life,
and tell them to weep.

SHIPMATE
    Why should they cry?

ODYSSEUS
    Because the winds sweep us along now,
    sweep us north and south and west.
    And Ithaca lies east.

SHIPMATE
    But we're almost home. I saw trees, landmarks, fires
        burning above the coast. It was close enough to touch.

ODYSSEUS
    But you were thieves instead. Now wave goodbye.

The wind-speed increases, howling across the ship.

SHIPMATE
    No. No. (*screams*) ITHACA. ITHACA . . .

ODYSSEUS (*almost to himself*)
    Tell it to the stars. Save your tonsils.
    Ithaca sails away. She can't hear you.

IN THE PALACE OF THE PHAEACIANS

NAUSICAA
I can't bear it.
To have smelt the pine cones of your own country,
only to be yanked away. Such cruelty.

ALCINOUS
Weren't you tempted to dive in and swim for it?

ODYSSEUS
In that maelstrom
I would have drowned instantly, disappeared completely.
And I was half-tempted, for that very reason, to be shot
of the whole thing, to shut out the torture, to end it
there and then. After all, the Gods can't torment the
    dead,
can they? But instincts took over. The will to live –
it's an impulse that can't be repressed. And I took
    comfort
in one thing: the winds whipped up such surf and
    spindrift
that Ithaca couldn't be seen. How sad would that have
    been –
to watch the home fires of my home town receding?

No, desolated but too numb to be defeated, I clung on.
We were blown back to where we'd begun, the Island
of Aeolia, but this time Aeolus shunned us, turned us
    away,
saying, 'The Gods never want you to rest, Odysseus,
there's a hex on your head. I shouldn't help you again,
they might turn their anger on me. Get out of my life.'

NAUSICAA
  So you sailed again? Where to next?

ODYSSEUS
  To where the breeze took us – Laestrygonia.
  That land of endless sun, with less than a hair's breadth
  between dusk and daybreak, where night-time
  is the split-second blink of heaven's eyelid.

  It should have been a routine stop for supplies,
  so I moored my vessel some distance off at sea.
  The fleet sailed into the narrow-jawed harbour
  and a search party followed a twist of smoke
  to where a thick-limbed girl drew water from a well.
  Follow me home, she told them. They followed.
  In the halls of the Laestrygonians sat her mother,
  a giant toad of a woman. She called her husband,
  Antiphates, king of those people. I say people,
  I mean people-eaters. He snatched one of my men,
  swallowed him whole. The rest ran for the boats
  but the cannibals followed, hundreds now,
  stoning the boats from the headland
  and hunting my men like spear-fishermen.
  'Row for your lives, row for your lives,' I bellowed.
  I hauled three or four floundering men aboard,
  slit the mooring ropes with my sword
  and my boat pulled clear. But not the others.

  Not one ship made it out of that harbour.

  If twelve ships sailed from Troy for Ithaca,
  now we were one vessel alone, and heartbroken.

  Behind us, planks, clothing and limbs
  floated randomly on the crimson ocean.

We pin-balled between islands again, barely conscious.
We were lost utterly. Knew nothing. Cared even less.

But after slaughter came humiliation and ignominy:
the wind delivered us into the lap of Circe.

CIRCE

Odysseus and the last of his men on land on Aeaea. They are seated around a campfire, eating a meal on the beach.

ELPENOS

This is the sweetest food.

EURYBATES

Yes, stag. I feel big when I've eaten stag.

ELPENOS

I know what you mean – as if you've eaten its spirit as well. As if the ghost of the stag enters the blood, making you fearless and proud. Like you're the king of the woods.

EURYBATES

I just meant it's very filling, that's all.

ELPENOS

Oh, I see.

EURYBATES

I was starving. I could have eaten the antlers as well. Very rich, though.

ELPENOS

Yes.

EURYBATES

Who killed it?

ELPENOS

Odysseus. Brought it down with one throw of the spear – thwack. Splintered its backbone. I saw him dragging it

down to the beach, hauling it on a rope made from
creepers and vines.

EURYBATES
Amazing.

ELPENOS
Yes, and he gave us the pick of the meat.

EURYBATES
Really generous.

ELPENOS
I feel terrible now after that business with the bag of wind
and everything we said.

EURYBATES
Me too.

ELPENOS
Yes, really rotten. Hey, are you leaving that rib?

EURYBATES
Have it. Very filling is stag. Very rich.

ODYSSEUS
Listen to me, men. I've been up on that crag
surveying the interior, trying to make a plan.
It's mysterious here. The plateau is dense jungle,
crammed with ancient trees that interweave
and link arms. Animal noises came to me,
but no beasts I could name from their voices.
I saw birds with feathers like flames, and plants
that swallowed insects, and lizards more like dragons
with double tongues and black smoking breath.

This is a disorienting place, no question of that.

In truth, it's hard to tell east from west,
or even dawn from dusk. The sea lies to every side.
To look for sweet water, animal flesh and fruit
we have no choice – we'll have to strike inland.

The men groan and protest.

ELPENOS
Haven't we learned our lesson by now?
Isn't there something of a pattern developing here?

POLITES
Hold your tongue.

ODYSSEUS
No, Polites, if he has something on his mind let him
speak.

ELPENOS
I'm not saying anything, all right. It's just that . . .

EURYBATES
He's saying we should just pack up and go. Every time we
go up country we come face to face with some bunch of
crazies trying to cut us to shreds, or some one-eyed
retard, or some other nightmare. Why don't we finish
our meal, get back on the boats and sail? At least on
the water there's only the weather to bother about.
What's a few thunderstorms compared with a
flesh-eating ogre, or flowers dosed with brain-addling
drugs, or blood-sucking primitives . . .?

ODYSSEUS
So it's fear, is it? Is that what roots you to the spot?

EURYBATES
Look what's happened to us! I've got every right to be

fearful. Yes, I'm afraid, and I don't mind saying so.
(*becoming tearful*) Terrified. Shit-scared, OK? Satisfied?
You're right, I should be used to it by now. My nerves
are shot. I'm finished.

ODYSSEUS
Well, even if your cowardice shames you,
some pride is salvaged by your honesty.
It's been desperate,
it's no surprise that cracks are starting to show.

But honesty doesn't change our predicament
or release us from jeopardy. It's no use blubbing.
And we can't sail without water and food,
we might as well slit our throats here on the beach.
So we soldier on. Here's my strategy:

There's no point putting the whole party at risk.
We divide into two groups, I'll lead one
and my good lord Eurylochus the other.

EURYLOCHUS
An honour, sir.

ODYSSEUS
We draw lots. One group remains here,
the other presses forward on reconnaissance.
Any dissenting voices to that plan of action?
Good. You, man, take off your helmet
and throw in these buttons – one gold,
one silver. Eurylochus, draw your lot.

*Two buttons are thrown into a bronze helmet. Eurylochus
draws out the gold one.*

EURYLOCHUS
    Gold, sir.

ODYSSEUS
    You win – that being the noblest of the metals.
    So, stand idle here by the ships, or cut a path into the
        bush
    and carve out a name for yourself? It's your choice.

EURYLOCHUS (*obliged to take on the challenge*)
    The choice is obvious.

ODYSSEUS
    Brave Eurylochus. Take two dozen men,
    and Polites, brother in arms, go with them.

POLITES
    I will. I'm ready for a change of scene.

ODYSSEUS
    Friends, death's door yawns open for us,
    but we won't enter, not for a while yet.
    These comrades of ours are our lifeline.
    Give them the best of your arrows and spears
    and press good luck into their handshakes.

    May the Gods of good fortune smile on you.
    We'll watch and listen for signs and signals.

*

*The reconnaissance party make their way through the
wooded interior of the island.*

ELPENOS
    Ouch!

EURYBATES
    What?

ELPENOS
    Mosquitoes.

EURYBATES
    I know, they're ravenous. I've given up counting the bites.
        I've got more bites than skin.

ELPENOS
    They can smell the fear. It's fear that attracts them.

EURYBATES
    Well, they must be having a feast day with me and I don't
        mind admitting it.

EURYLOCHUS
    Caution, men. Everybody keep low for a moment.

POLITES
    What is it?

EURYLOCHUS
    Look, in the clearing.

POLITES
    A magnificent palace. Only someone of great nobility
        could live there.

ELPENOS
    Or great cunning.

*A beguiling song drifts through the palace door and out
towards them.*

POLITES
    Listen.

EURYLOCHUS
What is it? Music?

POLITES
Singing. Hear it?

EURYLOCHUS
A woman's voice.

POLITES
Captivating. Enthralling. Enchanting.

They listen a while longer.

POLITES
We should . . . I'll take a handful of men and approach the
  gate.

EURYLOCHUS
I'll stay outside – take a look around the gardens and
  grounds.

POLITES
Listen to that voice – it's angelic. Inviting us in, almost.
Anyway, we can't just go on skulking in the bushes.
We might as well take the initiative.
You others, come with me, but there's a lady at home,
so mind your manners.

*They approach the door. The singing is louder and more
beautiful than ever.*

ELPENOS
I haven't heard singing like that for years.

EURYBATES
There's no more wonderful instrument than the human

voice. My wife used to sing to me while she was cutting
my hair.

ELPENOS
My daughter was the singer in our house. A little song-
bird, she was. She won't be little any more. She'll have
flown the nest.

POLITES
All right, make yourselves presentable, men.
Keep your weapons close to hand but no sudden moves.
We don't want a bloodbath.

*He bangs on the door. The singing continues inside the
house. Polites knocks again. The singer reaches the end of
the song and stops. Slow, measured footsteps make their way
towards the door, accompanied by the swishing hem of a
long dress. The door opens.*

CIRCE (*seductively*)
Hello, gentlemen.

POLITES
Forgive our intrusion.

CIRCE
What's to forgive? I can sing any time,
but it's not every day a band of men call at my door.
Were you washed ashore?

POLITES
We've been blown every which way –
will you excuse our untidy appearance?

CIRCE
I see only the potential in a man, not his blurred outline.
But don't loiter in the doorway, gentlemen. Come in.

They file into the house and are shown into a dining room.

CIRCE

    Does any one of you men have an appetite?

ELPENOS

    What a spread. There's enough here to feed an army.

POLITES

    This is . . . an unexpected surprise.

EURYBATES

    Oh, brother, I think my belly's going to leap up through
       my throat and lunge for it. Er, if you'll pardon my way
       of speaking, ma'am.

CIRCE

    Do be seated. Don't stand on ceremony.

POLITES

    And just the right number of chairs. It's as if you were
       expecting us.

CIRCE

    Never underestimate the foresight of the hostess.

EURYBATES

    No, don't do that, Polites. And don't look a gift-horse in
       the mouth either.

ELPENOS

    There's wine by the gallon. And food I've never seen the
       likes of. Dishes I don't even recognize.

CIRCE

    You look like men of the world.
    You don't look like men who'd turn down a meal
    just because it was foreign or unfamiliar.

ELPENOS
    Too right we wouldn't.

EURYBATES (*tucking in*)
    So you keep a bit of a farm, do you? I noticed the stalls in
        the walled garden.

CIRCE
    I have livestock – it's true.

EURYBATES
    I have a few sheep myself at home, and a couple of goats.

CIRCE
    Fascinating.

EURYBATES
    And a pig. An old grunter. Mind you, he'll be bacon
        by now.

CIRCE
    Won't you take off your cloak and be seated, Captain?

POLITES
    I saw . . . I just thought I . . . is that a wolf in the garden?

CIRCE
    She-wolf. Female. But that's a male. See him – curled
        under the magnolia tree. He's a beauty, isn't he?

POLITES
    That's . . . a lion.

CIRCE
    Captain, you do know your natural history.

POLITES
    Aren't they . . . aggressive?

CIRCE

On the contrary. They're my puppies. My kittens.
There's no violence here. Give me your hand –

She places his hand over her heart.

Can't you feel the calmness, the peace, the delight . . .

POLITES (*seduced*)

Forgive me. It's been such a long time.

CIRCE

Here, drink all of this, before your men empty the cellar.

He downs a full glass of the wine-potion.

POLITES

Absolute nectar. Thank you.

CIRCE (*to Eurybates*)

So you were saying you kept animals of the porcine
variety.

EURYBATES

Say what?

ELPENOS

She's asking if you keep pigs.

EURYBATES

Oh, right. Just the one. A big porker he was, with a
SQUOINK! Oh, pardon my manners, ma'am. Must be
the wine. Haven't tasted such SQUOINK! SQUOINK!

ELPENOS

You can't hold your drink – you're an embarrassment.
Do ignore him, he's such a pig. Not fit to go GROINK!
GROINK! GROINK!

EURYBATES

Are you taking the SQUOINK! SQUOINK! Don't laugh
at me – you've got a snout instead of a SQUOINK!
SQUOINK! SQUOINK! SQUOINK!

ELPENOS

Think that's funny? You've – GROINK! GROINK!
GROINK! – got a tail growing out of your GROINK!
GROINK!

EURYBATES

SQUOINK! GROINK! Hey, what's – GRUNK!
GRUNK! – going on?

ELPENOS

GRRRRRRRUUUUUOOOOIIIIIINNNNNK! Help!
Captain!

CIRCE

Oh, he's got problems of his own. He can't help you, can
you, Captain?

POLITES

SSQQQQQQQQQUUUUUUUUUUEEEEEEEEEAAAA . . .

*

Eurylochus bursts through the woods onto the beach.

EURYLOCHUS

Odysseus, help. We're bewitched.

ODYSSEUS

Catch your breath. Say what's happened.

EURYLOCHUS

Evil magic and dark mystery. A woman singing –

an exquisite voice, I felt my heart melting.
She invited them in for supper and drink.
I watched through the window. Odysseus,
she's beautiful, breathtaking. Suddenly
one of the men put down his goblet of wine
and there on the front of his face was a . . .

ODYSSEUS
A what?

EURYLOCHUS
A snout –
not a nose but a snout, and out of his mouth
fell a long, rough, disgusting, lolloping tongue . . .

SHIPMATE
Sounds like he's been at the drink himself!

EURYLOCHUS
NO – I sensed a trap and waited outside.
Not one drop of intoxicant has passed my lips.

ODYSSEUS
I'm afraid I believe you. Tell us what else.

EURYLOCHUS
Another man reached forward for a piece of fruit
and . . . and out popped a pink curly tail from the base
of his spine. And there at the end of his cuffs,
instead of hands – two dirty big hooves.
But Odysseus, she's beautiful, so beautiful . . .

ODYSSEUS
This could only be the woman they call Circe.
It's her magic they've fallen for. And what of Polites –
is he spellbound as well? Did he drink the brew?

EURYLOCHUS
    He dropped to the floor with the rest,
    snuffled among the crumbs on all fours
    while the witch herded them outside into a sty,
    laughing madly at her wicked trick.
    Where he once had a handsome face
    he now has jowls and two white tusks.

ODYSSEUS
    It's Circe's work – no question. I should have guessed.
    I should have gone myself in the first place.
    Which direction is the palace? I'll have to find a way
    to unwork this magic of hers before it sticks.

EURYLOCHUS
    Head for the heart of the island if you must.
    The gardens and grounds crawl with wild beasts –
    lions and wolves – but they nuzzle at your hands,
    roll over at your feet. They're doped.
    There's dark practice at work in that manor.
    But she's so beautiful, so beautiful . . .

ODYSSEUS
    Guard the ship.
    And if a tiger or bear or wild boar
    comes crashing onto the beach later today,
    don't cut out its heart for sacrifice, or light a fire
    and dish it out as meat – it might be me.

                                    *

*On his way to Circe's palace, Odysseus senses a presence
near by.*

ODYSSEUS

Who is it? Don't hide in the bushes, coward,
step onto the path and make yourself known.

HERMES

You'll know me soon enough, and then you'll give
thanks.

ODYSSEUS

Come out of the undergrowth, or I'll hack into it.

HERMES

You'd wave your sword at a God, Odysseus?

ODYSSEUS

God? What God? You're a servant of the witch.

HERMES

I serve only Zeus. Cast your eyes over me, Odysseus.
Who has wings at his feet and carries a golden staff?

ODYSSEUS

Only the God Hermes.

HERMES

Then look at the God Hermes.

ODYSSEUS

I . . . why would a God meet Odysseus on such a lonely
path?

HERMES

Hermes – the God of travellers, guide in the wilderness –
where else should you meet him but such a place?
Now look again at him and listen to his voice.

Your friends are held behind a gate in Circe's pens –
transformed into pigs. You rush towards them

hoping to set them free, but do exactly as I say,
word for word, or you'll suffer the same fate.

ODYSSEUS

Forgive my ignorance, Hermes. I put away my sword.

HERMES

Do that. It isn't a weapon you need but a plant.

ODYSSEUS

To offer to Circe? To flatter her with, or to trade?

HERMES

To keep to yourself. She'll hand you a slug of wine –
drink it back. It's the same potion that turned your men
to swine. Drink it down – right to the last drop.

ODYSSEUS

Then what? Wait for hooves to appear at my wrists?

HERMES

There's a rare flower that grows here in the grass.
The moly. Track it down and pluck it from its bed.
You'll know it when you see it. The stem is black,
and its black roots have a tight grip on the earth.
But its petals are white. Vibrant, incandescent white.

In your possession that flower will keep you safe.
You'll be inoculated, resistant to the drug
and any other devilment or spell she throws your way.

Repel her. Then draw your sword, and she'll do as you say.

ODYSSEUS

Show me where this moly flower grows.

HERMES

I'm not here to lead you by the nose, Odysseus,

only to whisper a word or two of advice.
Find it yourself. Grub it out. Remember, black
at the root and stem, petals incandescent white.

Black at the root and stem, petals incandescent white . . .

*

Odysseus enters Circe's palace later.

CIRCE
And here's the handsomest warrior of them all.

ODYSSEUS
Where are my men?

CIRCE
Having fun. You're very tense, here in the shoulders
and the neck. Why don't you relax?

ODYSSEUS
I've come for my men.

CIRCE
Are you sure? Are you sure it isn't a woman you're
looking for?

ODYSSEUS
We're sorry to have disturbed you.
We're just passing through, looking for supplies.

CIRCE
Then help yourself to whatever you see.
Doesn't this delicious-looking food tempt you?

ODYSSEUS
I'll only eat when the rest of the crew can be fed.

CIRCE

Then a drink. Who would begrudge you a drink?
Here, the sweetest wine ever to touch your lips.
Taste it. Let it loose on your tongue.
Let it loose in your blood.

Odysseus drains the glass.

Ha! You're a thirsty swine. Now get to the sty with the
rest of the litter.

ODYSSEUS

I think not. I won't be eating from any trough, Circe.

CIRCE

What! You'll not resist me.
Be a pig, I say. Be a pig.

ODYSSEUS

I hear no squealing or grunts.

CIRCE

BE A PIG. BE A PIG.

ODYSSEUS

I feel no long floppy ears. I see no sprouting tail.

CIRCE (*She beats his chest.*)
PIG, PIG. PIG, PIG.

ODYSSEUS (*He grabs her by the neck, half-choking her, and
draws his sword*).
What sort of hog could handle a weapon, like this pig
can?
Rest the blade – just so – on the butcher's neck?
What name will you give to this beast?

CIRCE
   You . . . you're Odysseus. Here in my house!
   Hermes predicted you'd come one day,
   with your twisting words like a box of snakes.

   With your . . . iron strength, your quick tongue, your
      golden face . . .

ODYSSEUS
   And how accurate he was. How truthful and precise.

CIRCE (*suddenly passionate*)
   Odysseus, I can't tell you how long I've brooded on this.
   Other men turn to low, pathetic creatures in my eyes,
   but you resist, you resist. Come to my bed, Odysseus . . .

ODYSSEUS
   One minute she's sending me to the farmyard,
   the next she's pulling me under the sheets . . .

CIRCE
   We'll make magical love, Odysseus.
   We'll bring our powers together, pool our strength.
   Mix with me, Odysseus. Let your limbs tangle with mine,
   let your thoughts become mine.
   (*whispers*)
   You'll fuck me, Odysseus . . .

ODYSSEUS
   You'll show me some courtesy, Circe.

   I'll eat and drink with you, take
   some of the delicacies you offer.
   What hungry man could resist such a feast?

   But first, unlock my men from the pens,
   and wave your wand over their heads.

Then swear you'll keep your magic to yourself,
and swear you'll help us in our journey home.

CIRCE
　I do, I do.

ODYSSEUS
　Once every ounce of rind on their backs
　is restored to flesh, and they stand upright
　and speak with a human voice, then I'll taste
　a little of what you spread in front of me.
　But first swear. Swear on your life.

CIRCE
　I promise, Odysseus. I swear.

IN THE PALACE OF THE PHAEACIANS

ALCINOUS
   And did they regain their human form?

ODYSSEUS
   They did. And then they washed,
   scrubbed till their skin was raw,
   trying to scour away the smell of pig,
   spitting the taste of pig from their throats,
   coughing pig out of their lungs.

ARETE
   And the herb went on keeping you from harm?

ODYSSEUS
   Its powers went deeper than any witch's spell.

NAUSICAA
   And afterwards I presume you told that scheming,
   conniving hostess of yours to go to Hades on a horse and
      cart?
   Or even lopped off her head with your sword?

ODYSSEUS
   No, it was . . . I judged it more complicated than that.
   The men were in need of rest and shelter.

NAUSICAA
   How could you stay, even for another hour?

ODYSSEUS
   It took upwards of a week to stitch the sail . . .

NAUSICAA
   You loitered there for a week?

ODYSSEUS
And while the boat was beached we took the chance
to smoke the sea-worms out of the hull, re-caulk the
    prow,
bolster the keel – that took a month . . .

NAUSICAA
You'll be saying next you waited a full season
for the weather to change . . .

ODYSSEUS
In fact before we knew it a year had slipped by . . .

NAUSICAA
A year! You must have dined many times at her table,
    Odysseus.
You must have been one satisfied guest!

ARETE
Finally my daughter sees the other side of him!

ODYSSEUS
Circe restored our spirits.

NAUSICAA
I don't doubt it for a minute.

ARETE
We're women. We know what this smacks of.

ODYSSEUS
I can see where that line of thought might lead.
But I had to consider the men:
when we landed they were bone-weary
and half-drowned. Their eyes carried no light.
Months at sea had turned their fingers to rope
and their brains to salt. Whenever they spoke

it was only to curse or to plot mutiny.
They needed fattening up and thawing out.
They needed to rest. It took twelve long months.

LEAVING *ACHAEA*

A year has passed since Odysseus and his men first arrived.

CIRCE
I know what you're going to say.

ODYSSEUS
My men plead with me night and day. They long for
home.

CIRCE
Then they can go.
But you could stay, Odysseus. You could live with me
here.

ODYSSEUS
I could. But my heart begs me to leave.

CIRCE
Think of the times we've had.
We've bathed in the sacred streams.
Lazed in the afternoons on cushions of purple silk.
Eaten from silver plates.
Sipped wine from gold cups.

ODYSSEUS
Circe . . .

CIRCE (*whispering*)
We've fallen asleep together under the stars,
woken on thick fleeces,
taken whatever we pleased,
wanted for nothing . . .

ODYSSEUS

With every day that passes it gets harder to leave . . .

CIRCE

Whatever you've asked for, I've given.
It's all yours, Odysseus.
Why deny what you most desire . . .

POLITES (*from afar*)

Odysseus, the wind fills the sails.
The men are waiting for orders. Odysseus?

CIRCE

Odysseus, Odysseus . . .
You've feasted on fantasy with me. You still want more.
You crave me . . .

ODYSSEUS

You whisper your magic in my ear.
You swore an oath.

CIRCE

You'll tear my heart out if you leave.
And you'll leave your own heart here with me.

ODYSSEUS

If I stay you'll have broken your word.
What will I feel about you then?

POLITES (*calling*)

Odysseus? Odysseus?

CIRCE

Go, then, if you must.
But travel first to the Land of the Dead,
speak with Tiresias. Even as a blind corpse
he has the Gift. Seek him out. Hear his advice.

ODYSSEUS

How does a living mortal enter the Land of the Dead?

CIRCLE

There's no map, only a current. An undertow.

ODYSSEUS

To the wooded coast?

CIRCE

Into the flooded forest. Do you know the journey?

ODYSSEUS

I've heard tell but never believed it.
Through the groves of Persephone?

CIRCE

Between and amongst the black poplars.
And past the trees of dying fruit.
Stinking things, heavy with rot. Beyond those.
To a shore where leaf-mould and decay
make it difficult to breathe. Anchor the boat
and walk to the spit where two rivers
curdle and merge. To one side there's a bluff,
a looming, swaying, overhanging rock . . .

Go. Cast off. I'll stand on the cliff,
watching you out of sight.
You'll feel my nails in your back,
taste the blood of my last kiss.

THE KINGDOM OF THE DEAD

ODYSSEUS

This way, under the crag. This is the way she described.
Eurylochus and Polites, accompany me.

EURYLOCHUS

If the dead come here, then may the Gods keep me alive.
The agony and humiliation of old age has nothing on this.
I'll hold my dying breath, I'll cling to life by my
    fingernails.

POLITES

The air reeks. The breeze carries a sour breath.

ODYSSEUS

Here in the river sand, help me dig a pit, just as Circe
    said.
About an elbow's length in each direction and a span
    deep.

EURYLOCHUS

I'll chop out the gravel with my sword and rake it aside.

ODYSSEUS

Polites, did you bring the libations?

POLITES

I have them here.

ODYSSEUS

Pass them in order, as she instructed.

Speaking into the void, he pours each liquid into the pit in
turn.

Here's drink for the dead. Succulent honey blended with
    milk.
And here's drink for the dead. Sweet wine from the pick
    of the vines.
And here's drink for the dead. Pure water from the
    mountain stream.

EURYLOCHUS
And now the grain, Odysseus.

ODYSSEUS
And here's the seed of the field, a scatter of barley.

And on my return to Ithaca, I swear to slaughter
the prime bull of the herd in the name of the dead,
and light a bonfire of treasure to you, Tiresias.

POLITES
See how the liquid bubbles and stews.

ODYSSEUS
Now the blood.

EURYLOCHUS
You men, bring the sheep.

*The men manhandle the scuffling and bleating sheep towards
the pit.*

The ram first. Hold it firm on its side – there, at the pit.
I'll bare its throat for your sword, Odysseus.

ODYSSEUS (*calling into the void again*)
And here's rich, dark blood for the dead.

*He draws his sword and cuts the animal's throat. Blood
spurts and pours into the pit.*

[138]

EURYLOCHUS
Now the black ewe. Don't fight it, Polites.
Don't break its neck before the blade takes its life.
Ready, Odysseus.

ODYSSEUS (*to the ghosts*)
Rouse yourselves. Come gather round this purple pool
which overflows in your name. Be drawn to the blood.

*The blood of the black ewe gushes into the pit. The
harrowing wails and moans of the dead start up in the
distance, coming nearer.*

Look – now they flock to me, the dead.
Up out of Hades they come,
the souls of the departed.
Unhappy crowd, sorrowful mob.
Young brides, unmarried boys,
babes who died in the cot,
old men who perished alone,
women with their hearts weeping,
battalions of men who died at war,
some still in their battledress,
some still with their shields raised.
Look how they swarm
like bats from a cave.
See how this puddle of blood
attracts them from the grave.
Pitiful, pitiful the massed ranks
of the lost, restless in death.
A million troubled, weightless ghosts.

EURYLOCHUS (*frightened*)
Keep them at bay with your sword.
Swish it through the air.

POLITES
No, dip the sword in the blood
and call out Tiresias by name.

ODYSSEUS (*He dips his sword in the blood-filled pit, and
calls out.*)
I offer blood on my blade.
Tiresias – I offer blood on my blade.

TIRESIAS
Who disturbs Tiresias?
Who stirs him from his sleep?

ODYSSEUS
I . . . Odysseus.

TIRESIAS
Odysseus, is it? Come to pick my brains.

ODYSSEUS
Here's fresh blood. Drink as much as you please.

TIRESIAS
Cruel and cunning, Odysseus. No ghost
can resist the taste of liquid flesh.
No soul can refuse communion with the living wine.
(*He laps at the blood.*)
Still warm. Still warm.

ODYSSEUS
One question, Tiresias – will I ever reach home?

TIRESIAS
Ha! That's what brings you here, is it . . .
slumming it with the bone brigade . . .
I'll tell you this much . . . Poseidon won't rest.

You burnt out his son's eye – now he's hell-bent on
   revenge.
But will you reach home? You might . . .
Can you restrain the crude desires of your men? – that's
   the question.
Can you restrain your own?
(*entering a vision-state*)
I see . . . the Island of Thrinacia . . .
I see the Sun God, Helios – his herd – the Cattle of the
   Sun –
prime, graceful, docile
– their limbs thick with beef.
Swallow your appetite . . . leave them to graze.
Leave that slow, lumbering herd in peace,
and you might see Ithaca again.
But harm them in any way . . . I see broken ships . . .
   broken friends . . .
I see your house, Odysseus, your wife Penelope
besieged by coarse, rapacious men
. . . a house of suffering . . . I see . . . I see . . . the vision
   fades.

POLITES

   But another comes forward – a woman. Who is it?

EURYLOCHUS

   I can't tell – it's nothing more than a shade.

ODYSSEUS

   Come forward. Approach the blood.

POLITES

   Oh, the Gods help poor Odysseus. I know that shape.

EURYLOCHUS

   Oh, you poor, bedevilled man. My poor, tortured king.

ODYSSEUS
    Is it . . .
    Is it . . .
    . . . mother . . .?

ANTICLEIA
    Oh, my beautiful boy, still alive.

ODYSSEUS
    Mother, why are you here with these shabby ghosts?
    These phantoms are no company for your living heart.

ANTICLEIA
    Not living, Odysseus. This heart has stopped.

ODYSSEUS (*grief-stricken*)
    No . . . No . . .

ANTICLEIA
    There's no pulse, now. No strength
    to take my beautiful boy in my arms.

ODYSSEUS
    But I left you happy and well.
    (*angry*)
    Who tricked you into this long sleep?
    Who shall I hunt down in revenge?
    Who'll pray to highest heaven that he never lived?

ANTICLEIA
    Not murder, Odysseus. Not foul play.

ODYSSEUS
    Then how? You were too young in years
    to just close your eyes and die.

ANTICLEIA

    I died of grief for my son.
    For you, Odysseus. I died for you.

    Once a woman bears a child
    her heart's no longer her own.
    When that child is lost,
    so is the will to go on.
    Grief for the missing is worse
    than grief for the dead.

    I died of longing, Odysseus.
    I died of my love for you.

    And your wife, Penelope – she waits.
    She waits in Ithaca – dying the same death.

ODYSSEUS

    No! This is an optical trick.
    The Gods have twisted me one way, then another;
    they're out to deceive me – this is their latest illusion.

ANTICLEIA

    No, my Odysseus, what you see is truth.
    This is what happens once death has made its choice.

    The blood drains. The nerves become numb.
    Flesh won't cling to the scaffold of bones.

    The heat of life cools to a powdery ash.
    The bird of the soul flies from its branch.

    (*Her voice begins to fade.*)
    Leave, now. Find the daylight that feeds you.
    Fight your way home to your wife.

ODYSSEUS (*calling into the darkness, sobbing*)
Mother, mother . . .

Odysseus falls to his knees in tears.

POLITES
Oh, beleaguered man. Sorrowful king. My heart weeps.

EURYLOCHUS
And here come other familiar faces.
Old comrades. Brothers in arms from Troy.

ODYSSEUS
Agamemnon? Agamemnon?

AGAMEMNON
Odysseus. Once we fought shoulder to shoulder.
Now I creep from the shadows to beg for blood
at your feet.

ODYSSEUS (*bewildered and tearful*)
Great leader. Proud and mighty soldier.

AGAMEMNON
Death makes me a vagrant and scavenger.

ODYSSEUS
Were you shipwrecked on the journey home?
Or ambushed by some rogue army?

AGAMEMNON
Nothing as proud as that.
Not killed in battle or crushed by Poseidon's fist.

Murdered! Worse – murdered by my wife
and her lover. Cut down in my own house.
While we battled for Troy, she rolled in the sheets.
While we defended our lives, she opened her legs.

When I returned, victorious, exhausted,
succulent food was prepared. Stabbed in the back
I died face-down in the fruits and breads and meats
of my own homecoming feast.

ODYSSEUS
Disloyalty and deceit. Sick treachery.

AGAMEMNON
She brought shame on every woman and wife.
Beware of womankind, Odysseus. Not Penelope . . .
She was just a young bride when we sailed to war
with your new-born son at her breast.

POLITES
And yet another ghost. Another familiar face.

EURYLOCHUS
The vaults of death are rammed full with our friends.

ODYSSEUS
Achilles.

ACHILLES
You've wandered into the wrong territory, Odysseus.
You were always the luckiest man alive –
this is no place for the fortunate.
Everyone here has lost.

ODYSSEUS
Good Achilles, you're still my glorious nobleman,
my God-like lord.

ACHILLES
Praise is wasted here. It dies on the lips.
There are no leaders and no one to lead.
Make no mistake – this is the bitter end.

Does it appal? Does it look as bad as it feels?
Don't fall for the dream of the afterlife,
Odysseus. Live on as a maggot or worm
eating the dirt of the world or feeding on rancid meat.
Anything but this.

There's no glory in battle, no glorious death.
If I ever spoke of glorious death I take back those words.
Death and glory should never inhabit the same breath.

AGAMEMNON
But tell me of my son. Is he still alive?

ACHILLES
No, tell me about my boy first.

ODYSSEUS
Achilles, Agamemnon . . . what shall I say?

AGAMEMNON
Don't leave us in eternal doubt. Odysseus, please . . .

ACHILLES
Say something before it's too late. Cruel Odysseus.

ODYSSEUS
No, I . . .

POLITES
Look, the blood runs dry. They begin to fade.

The pleading voices of Agamemnon and Achilles fade away.

ACHILLES
Odysseus, please, please . . .

AGAMEMNON
Odysseus . . .

Odysseus is left weeping.

EURYLOCHUS
    Help me lift him.

They haul him to his feet.

    Lean on us, Odysseus.

    Let's flee this sinister watering hole.
    Who knows how many of our family and friends
    have entered the grave since we saw them last?
    Who knows which face might appear next from the dark?

IN THE PALACE OF THE PHAEACIANS

NAUSICAA
  Phaeacians – look with wonder on this sufferer,
  listen to his story. You doubted him at first,
  when I found him shivering in a nest of leaves.
  But his words resurrect him before our eyes.

ALCINOUS
  Odysseus, we mostly look on strangers with a cold stare.
  Fraudsters and tricksters have landed here,
  twisting their tongues into our ears.
  But you're no con man. You're too honest
  and open-hearted to be anything but true.
  I believe even my wife . . . Arete?

ARETE (*disturbed and moved*)
  The part with the mother . . .
  The mother dying of grief for her child . . .
  Meeting the mother beyond the grave . . . I found . . .
  I couldn't bear . . .

NAUSICAA
  You have the voice of a singer, Odysseus,
  and a poet's charm for bringing the past to life.
  We could listen all day and all night.

ODYSSEUS
  Then let me, in honour of my brave men,
  describe the final chapters of their lives.
  Men who fought and won the battle for Troy
  only to founder and fall on the journey home.

THE SIRENS

ODYSSEUS
Rest the oars for a moment while I talk.

POLITES (*shouts*)
Men, rest the oars.

ELPENOS (*under his breath*)
Here comes one of those big speeches.

ODYSSEUS
We're not drifting aimlessly, as some of you think.
We have a direction and a destination, and we're on
 course.
We didn't visit the Land of the Dead for no reason
but to take our bearings from the mouth of Tiresias.

ELPENOS (*whispering*)
Great, now we're getting instructions from a blind man.

EURYBATES
Yeah, and a dead one at that.

ODYSSEUS
We're bound for Thrinacia. It's a landmark.
And after that, it's only three or four short hops
from island to island before we reach our home,
our Ithaca.
But it's a hazardous route . . .

Groans from the crew.

Listen to me. Listen to what Tiresias said.
Your lives and my life are intertwined.
There's no unravelling the knot. Your lives

depend on mine – that's what this tangle means.
You'd do well to remember that. Bring me
a bowl of beeswax. We sail for Thrinacia.

ELPENOS
What did he ask for?

EURYBATES
Beeswax.

ELPENOS
What does he want beeswax for?

EURYBATES
Don't ask me. Maybe he's going to get down on his hands
and knees and polish the deck.

ELPENOS
Maybe he's lost the plot.

*

*They have sailed on for an hour or so when the wind begins
to drop.*

EURYBATES
Hey, feel that?

ELPENOS
What?

EURYBATES
The breeze.

ELPENOS
There isn't any. It's gone still.

EURYBATES
  That's right. That's what I mean.

POLITES
  Odysseus? Odysseus?

ODYSSEUS
  Has the sail gone limp?

POLITES
  Hanging like a veil. There isn't a breath of air.

ODYSSEUS
  Assemble the crew.

A faint singing begins in the faraway distance, then fades.

  There isn't much time.

POLITES (*shouts*)
  Everyone in line, double quick.

The men assemble on deck.

ODYSSEUS
  Men, we're making good headway,
  but the Island of the Sirens looms.

  On pain of death, don't let their songs
  enter your head. Here's beeswax for your ears –
  I've kneaded it all afternoon in the sun.
  Here, every one of you, take a gobbet,
  and when I give the signal
  bung it deep in your lugs. Good.

  Now get the strongest rope on board
  and lash me tightly to the mast . . .
  Bind me in coils of rope.

POLITES
    Sir, we wouldn't dream of roping you like a wild horse . . .

ODYSSEUS
    And then row and row and row.
    Dig into the waves as if you were drunk
    and digging for gold. No – tunnelling
    out of a grave. As if you were buried alive.
    And whatever I say, however much I scream
    or threaten or plead – ignore every word.

    Is that clear?

    So do it. NOW.

They lash him to the mast

ODYSSEUS
    Now bung your ears with the wax, and row for your lives.

*A silence descends. The noise of the men and the sound of
the waves gradually disappear. The song of the Sirens enters
Odysseus' head.*

SIRENS
    Here where the fires burn . . .
    Here where the stars glow . . .
    Here where the fruits grow . . .
    Here where the heart turns . . .
        Come, Odysseus. Odysseus, come . . .

ODYSSEUS (*moaning*)
    This is witchery . . . but pleasant. Soothing.

SIRENS
    Here where the fires glow . . .
    Here where the stars turn . . .

Here where the fruits burn . . .
Here where the heart grows . . .
    Come, Odysseus. Odysseus, come . . .

ODYSSEUS

This music touches me. It has fingers and hands.
I feel its breath. I feel its mouth. Oh . . .

SIRENS

Here where the fires turn . . .
Here where the stars grow . . .
Here where the fruits glow . . .
Here where the heart burns . . .
    Come, Odysseus. Odysseus, come . . .

ODYSSEUS

Men, put down your work and untie me.
Listen, listen to the pull of it, the pull of it . . .

SIRENS

Here where the fires grow . . .

ODYSSEUS

. . . fires grow . . .

SIRENS

Here where the stars burn . . .
Here where the fruits turn . . .

ODYSSEUS

. . . where the . . . where the . . .

SIRENS

Here where the heart glows . . .

ODYSSEUS

. . . where the heart glows . . .

SIRENS AND ODYSSEUS
Come, Odysseus. Odysseus, come . . .

ODYSSEUS
Sail nearer to the shore – that's an order.
Men, angels are calling us – don't ignore them.
All my treasures are yours if you take me closer.
Untie me, I'll stab any man who disobeys me.
Eurylochus, friend, slit these ropes with a blade.
Men – a woman for every one of us – they promise us.
Polites, I command you to sail towards that chorus.
Untie me now. Now. Untie me, you bastard scum.
Zeus, hear me. I'll sacrifice everything in your name.
All my flocks and herds, all my land and estates . . .
All my servants and slaves . . . these men . . . take
them . . .
(*desperate*)
My son, Telemachus . . . my wife, Penelope . . .
(*sobbing*)
Take them all, but guide me into these voices . . .
Zeus, kill me afterwards, but show me their faces . . .

I CAN'T LIVE WITHOUT KISSING THE MOUTHS
OF THE SIRENS.

*He wails and moans as the ship passes the island and the
music dies away in the distance.*

SCYLLA AND CHARYBDIS

Later. Odysseus comes to with the men standing around him.

ODYSSEUS
Is it over?

POLITES
Some time ago. You passed out.

ODYSSEUS
The singing, what if it starts up . . .

EURYLOCHUS
We're out of earshot. We thought it safe to untie you.

ODYSSEUS
Eurylochus, and you, my faithful Polites.
Wild thoughts came into my mind,
loose words came out of my mouth . . .

EURYLOCHUS
We couldn't hear you.

POLITES
Beeswax – remember.

ODYSSEUS
Then let the Gods forgive me,
for they surely heard.

POLITES
But why did you put yourself through it?
You could have plugged your ears like the rest of us.

EURYLOCHUS

He's the only man to have heard the sirens and lived.
Isn't that right, Odysseus? One more claim to fame.

POLITES

It's all in the past now.
Let's pray for plain sailing.

An almighty burst of thunder booms across the ocean.

SHIPMATE

Look out, rocks up ahead.

EURYLOCHUS

What is it – a reef of some kind?

SHIPMATE

Some form of narrow channel between two islands.

POLITES

A crag on one side and a cliff on the other.
Do we sail through it, Odysseus? What's the order?

ODYSSEUS

Achaeans – clench your hearts into fists.
We've lived through danger time and time again.

EURYLOCHUS

A trench of fuming water – it that our passageway?

ODYSSEUS

Don't feel small and weary, men.
Feel battle-hardened – toughened and tempered
by the heat of skirmish and war.

POLITES

And the wind – it's dropped to a dead calm. Should we
turn about?

ODYSSEUS
  There'll be no doubling back –
  the way home lies straight ahead.
  Oarsmen, strike the waves
  with a strong, quiet beat and don't flinch.
  Don't lift your heads until we're through.

EURYLOCHUS
  What do you know that we don't?

ODYSSEUS
  Two perils.
  On the port side – a whirlpool. Charybdis!
  Three times a day she opens her throat
  and swallows the sea, sucks all and sundry
  into a burning, sulphurous pit. Enter that vortex
  and we'll never see the light of day again.
  No wooden craft could survive her gullet.
  Ships that have used the trailing fig tree
  on the rocky crag as a marker or flag
  have been dragged down into her guts.
  She vomits the bones of sea-dragons and whales.

POLITES
  Then we'll steer clear.

EURYLOCHUS
  Tilt the rudder. Men, make for the starboard cliff.

ODYSSEUS
  No – on that side there's a greater evil.
  See the mouth of that cave, draped in mist.
  Six-headed Scylla sleeps in its depth.
  A writhing mass of limbs, she reeks of death.
  Each neck of hers is a tentacle, each of her heads

a killing machine – three racks of teeth to every jaw.
Wake her, and we'll be mince in her mouth.

EURYLOCHUS
So we're done for.

ODYSSEUS
Not if we hold our nerve.
Oarsmen – keep on with that muffled stroke.
A swift, straight course and we'll cheat both these perils.
Be metal-headed and iron-hearted, men.
Don't swerve from the task.

SHIPMATE
Sir, something stirs in the cave.

ODYSSEUS
Hold your course.

SHIPMATE
It's heard us. Look, there in the mist. It's . . . hideous.

ODYSSEUS
Hold your course.

POLITES
Steer the other way.

EURYLOCHUS
No, not to this side.
A black hole opens up – look – a steaming abyss –
the sea pours into it.
Keep away from the brink.
Pull to the other side.

ODYSSEUS
Oarsmen – harder now, and faster.

SHIPMATE

We're trapped. We've sailed into the mouth of death.

ODYSSEUS

Hold your course.

POLITES

The monster. She's looming over the cliff, waiting to pick
us off.
Do something, Odysseus.

ODYSSEUS

Row harder and straighter. Heads down. Eyes forward.

EURYLOCHUS

Keep to starboard – we're being sucked in.

SHIPMATE

I can smell her breath. Heave to port. No . . . Here she
comes.

POLITES

Load up with arrows and spears – fire at will.

ODYSSEUS

Don't inflame her. Hold your course, I say.

POLITES

We won't die without a fight. Let fly, men, let fly.

Arrows are loosed off, spears fly through the air.

SHIPMATE

They bounce off her flesh. Now she's on the rampage.

EURYLOCHUS

Heave away – we're too close to the edge.

SHIPMATE
No . . . No . . . Save us. Save us.

The men scream as Scylla's six heads whip through the air,
snatching oarsmen out of the boat.

POLITES
We're defenceless.

SHIPMATE
Six men plucked from their seats.

POLITES
She slithers back to her cave, one in each mouth.

SHIPMATE
We'll never see them again.
They're hers for life now – hopeless prisoners.

POLITES
No – it's more savage than that.
Look, she gorges on them. Gulps them down.
Hammer the waves before she comes back for more.

SHIPMATE
Row – row – we'll be eaten alive.

EURYLOCHUS
Harder and faster – I think we're pulling clear.

Behind them, the six stricken men call out Odysseus' name
until their final breath.

ODYSSEUS (*forlornly*)
Hold your course. Heads down. Eyes forward. Hold your
    course.

THRINACIA

ODYSSEUS
And we praise those friends who are now lost.

MEN
Praise them.

ODYSSEUS
We salute their bravery and courage.

MEN
Salute them.

ODYSSEUS
We honour their families – those who are born of them,
those they were born from.

MEN
Honour them.

ODYSSEUS
And in their absence we grieve, and in grief
remember them.

MEN
Remember them.

ODYSSEUS
Raise the marker stone in their name
and sound the horn.

One long, steady note is blown softly from a conch.

ODYSSEUS
Let their souls rest. Let their troubles sleep.
(*changing tone*)

Men, we'll take refuge here for a while.
Mend the boat and tend to your wounds.
We're on the last leg, now. We're closing in on Ithaca.
It's time to start dreaming of home
and not be frightened of waking up.
It's within our grasp and it's real.
You're heroes – all of you – for making it this far.

But don't get too comfortable here.
Don't stray from the beach. Don't take what isn't yours.

EURYLOCHUS

    What do you mean?

ODYSSEUS

    Just keep your hands to yourself – that's all.

EURYLOCHUS

    You're a hard-nosed leader, Odysseus.

ODYSSEUS

    Explain that remark, Eurylochus.

EURYLOCHUS

    Look at us. What a rag-and-bone army we are.
    We've sailed with you for a decade now,
    zig-zagging between islands, drifting on the current.
    We've been mangled and battered at every turn.
    Look at us. We have broken limbs, smashed bones,
    ruptured organs, and our hearts . . .
    our hearts are utterly bent out of shape.

ODYSSEUS

    We've all suffered equally and the same.

EURYLOCHUS
 But your will is greater than ours. You're superhuman.
 You must be made out of stone by comparison.

ODYSSEUS
 What's this back-handed compliment leading to?

EURYLOCHUS
 It explains your coldness.
 Look around you – this is a land of plenty.

ODYSSEUS
 Don't lead the men astray with your rogue thoughts.

EURYLOCHUS
 Did you ever see such bounty?
 A herd of cattle grazes in fields above the coast –
 swaying through meadow grass, heavy with meat.
 Just one of those steers would feed us all . . .

ODYSSEUS
 Leave those cattle alone.

EURYLOCHUS
 But why shouldn't we eat?
 We're half-starved, half-drowned, half-alive,
 and you'd have us put back to sea on empty bellies.

ODYSSEUS
 Close your mutinous mouth.

EURYLOCHUS
 Just tell us why. Explain why we shouldn't feed.

ODYSSEUS
 You know why. You were there.

EURYLOCHUS
  Because Tiresias looked into his crystal ball?

ODYSSEUS
  You heard what he said.

EURYLOCHUS
  He'd have said anything for a taste of blood.

ODYSSEUS
  No, he's a seer of the future and a speaker of the truth.

EURYLOCHUS
  He was a blind old corpse. . . .

ODYSSEUS
  Are you sure it isn't yourself you think of, Eurylochus?
  It's you who has the taste of blood on his tongue,
  the smell of fried steak in his nose . . .

EURYLOCHUS
  Not true.

ODYSSEUS
  . . . the texture of roast beef between his teeth.
  It's you who'll say the first thing that comes into his head
  for a plate of meat.

EURYLOCHUS
  I'm only saying what everyone thinks . . .

ODYSSEUS
  You drooling fool.
  Are you Odysseus?

EURYLOCHUS
  That's a nonsense question.

[164]

ODYSSEUS
ARE YOU ODYSSEUS?

EURYLOCHUS
Of course not.

ODYSSEUS
No, and never imagine it – not for a split second.
Never dream of it. It's beyond anything you could
envisage.

Open your ears – the lot of you.
Those cows are the Cattle of the Sun.
Helios – the Sun God – they're his herd.
They never breed. They never die.
Leave them be and we'll be granted a safe passage home.
We'll follow Tiresias' prophecy to the word.
But spill one drop of their blood, pluck one bristle
from their hide, and you can kiss goodbye to Ithaca.
For ever.

This isn't advice – it's an order.
Now pack down for the night.
There's a storm brewing.

IN THE PALACE OF THE PHAEACIANS

ODYSSEUS
   That quelled them – for the time being.
   Unlike the weather. A storm twisted up from the sea,
   fanned by a wind from the south. The south wind –
   it blew for a month, never veering or letting up.
   It cornered us in the bay, kept us penned
   like sheep when the wolf howls at the gate.
   And breakers smashed against the cliff walls to all sides –
   to venture out would have been suicide.

   So we dug in, stayed put, eating the weeds
   that grew on the shore, bringing down gulls
   with crude arrows or stones, spearing the odd fish
   from the rocks, accepting whatever sea-life
   was thrown at our feet by the storm.

   My words had frightened the men.
   But fear doesn't last, and hunger
   has first call on the brain. There were rumblings.
   Murmurs. Men grumbling under their breath,
   behind their hands.

   Once the appetite starts to talk
   it's only a matter of time.

THE CATTLE OF THE SUN

A month has passed on Thrinacia. The men huddle around a fire, talking.

EURYLOCHUS
Is he asleep?

SHIPMATE
Snoring like a buffalo. A fly crawled across his face and he
didn't move.

POLITES
I still say we should hang fire – do as he says.

EURYLOCHUS
You didn't say that on the boat – when he told you not to
shoot.
Oh no, you picked up a bow and arrow and let fly.

POLITES
Yes, and look what happened.

EURYLOCHUS
You disobeyed him once – you can do it again.
That's the point I'm making.

POLITES
I just want to get home.

EURYLOCHUS
The same as everyone else does. Which is why it's time to
act.

SHIPMATE
Convince us, then. We're listening.

EURYLOCHUS

Men, I don't say these things lightly.
I've worshipped Odysseus from the very beginning.
I've followed him to the end of the earth – and half-way
    back.

But now I doubt his mind.
Face facts. We're starving to death,
and roaming free not more than a mile away
are a hundred head of prime beef.

It doesn't stack up. The equation doesn't work.

POLITES

So why doesn't he let us feast?

EURYLOCHUS

Superstition and delirium.
Tiresias in the underworld – Odysseus was truly spooked.
And seeing the ghost of his mother . . .
I think at that point he gave up.

SHIPMATE

As if he's risking our lives on purpose – is that what you
    mean?

EURYLOCHUS

As if some death-wish has entered his mind.

POLITES

You don't believe that. Do you?

EURYLOCHUS

Why else would he have steered into the teeth
of that six-headed beast, or tried to tip us
into that underwater hurricane?

No, comrades, we're in charge of our own destiny now.

There are thousands of roads that lead to death,
but starvation, that's the most painful route.
Torture – every inch. A slow, lingering demise.
I'd rather die at sea, crushed by Poseidon's fist,
than sit and watch my bones poke through my shrinking
    flesh.

SHIPMATE
   He's right. He's so right.

EURYLOCHUS
   Polites, what do you say?

POLITES
   It makes sense, the way you explain it.
   But I've got a bad feeling about this.

EURYLOCHUS
   Wait till you've got a decent meal inside you.
   You'll feel differently then.

POLITES
   I suppose.

EURYLOCHUS
   There's no suppose about it.
   Look – a full moon – she'll be our guide.
   It's still an hour before the Sun God rises.
   Round everyone up and hand out the spears.
   We're going hunting.

*

*The men gather at the edge of the pasture, talking in hushed
tones.*

EURYLOCHUS
Look at the width of the shoulders.

POLITES
And the haunches – think of the meat on those.

SHIPMATE
Yes, and look at the length of those horns.
I wouldn't want to be on the wrong end of one of those.

ELPENOS (*loudly*)
What's all the whispering about?

POLITES
We're trying to take them by surprise.
We don't want to chase them half-way over the mountain.

ELPENOS
You're kidding, aren't you? They're as soft as pudding.

SHIPMATE
A likely story.

ELPENOS
They're completely docile.

SHIPMATE
Those prongs don't look very docile.

ELPENOS
Look at him – he's seen us, but he's not fussed. Soft
article.

EURYLOCHUS
Prove it. Approach one of them.

ELPENOS
I will do. There's nothing to be afraid of.

[170]

SHIPMATE

    Here, take this spear.

ELPENOS

    You're not listening – I don't need one. Watch.

Elpenos sets off towards the cattle.

SHIPMATE

    He's either very brave or very stupid.

POLITES

    They've noticed him but they're not chasing him.

SHIPMATE

    What's he doing now?

POLITES

    He's touching it, pulling on its horns.

SHIPMATE

    Amazing – it's kneeling down for him.

ELPENOS (*his voice from afar*)

    Watch this then.

SHIPMATE

    What the . . . I've seen it all now.

POLITES

    He's riding it!
    He's climbed on its back and he's riding it like a pony.

ELPENOS (*coming closer, astride the cow*)

    Yee-ha! What did I tell you?

The bullock plods towards them.

SHIPMATE

It's unbelievable. It's . . . kind of beautiful.

POLITES

What do you say, Eurylochus?

EURYLOCHUS

Yes, a miracle. Now we know Odysseus was wrong.
This was meant to happen.

ELPENOS

Here we are, fellers. It's the only way to travel.
Beats sloshing around in a boat anyhow.

SHIPMATE

He's a magnificent animal.

POLITES

Quite awesome.

ELPENOS

Go on, stroke his nose. Feed him a clump of grass. Go on,
Eurylochus – he won't bite you.

EURYLOCHUS

An ironic statement, in the circumstances.

ELPENOS

What's he talking about?

EURYLOCHUS

Slide down from that hide, Achaean.

ELPENOS

What's the problem?

EURYLOCHUS

The problem is you're sitting astride about two tons of
raw beef.

You won't want it rolling on top of you.

Zeus, we thank you for your bounteous gifts.
Forgive us our hunger. Forgive us our sins.

He slits the creature's throat with a knife. It lets out a long, low death moan and slumps to the ground.

(*salivating and excited*)
Fetch buckets – don't loose the blood-soup.
Fetch a cleaver – hack it into quarters and build a fire on
    the beach.
Then slaughter another, then another, then another.
Protein – that's what we need to get home,
not hocus-pocus and mumbo-jumbo.

No human should starve while animals live.
It's unnatural. It's not how things were meant to be.

*

An hour or so later. Meat hisses and sizzles on a spit. The men laugh as they feast. Odysseus wakes with a start, sweating and talking to himself.

ODYSSEUS
    Eurylochus? Polites?

What a dream. I dreamed I was staked out
under the sun, the sun scorching my skin,
singeing my hair. Staked out till I caught fire.
What does it mean?

Eurylochus? Polites?

I need to cool down. I need to wash.

He walks to the shoreline and throws water at his face.

Oh, better. Better.
But I can still smell . . . What's that taste in the air?
(*suddenly panic-stricken*)
No, in the name of everything that matters –
tell me I'm mistaken.
(*shouting*)
Eurylochus? Polites?
(*approaching the camp fire*)
Tell me I'm wrong. Tell me this is a nightmare vision.

EURYLOCHUS
Relax, Odysseus.

ODYSSEUS
You disobeyed me.

EURYLOCHUS
Eat with us.
You'll agree with our actions once you've tasted this
    silverside.

ODYSSEUS
This is sacrilegious.

POLITES
We were all of one mind, Odysseus.
We respect your wishes, but our needs as humans have to
    come first.

EURYLOCHUS
Don't grovel. Stand your ground.

POLITES
I'm just explaining . . .

EURYLOCHUS
Don't explain and don't apologize.
No man should have to justify his need to eat.
No man should have to apologize for surviving –
not even to noble Odysseus.

ODYSSEUS
Greed and gluttony – they aren't the motives of civilized
men.

EURYLOCHUS
We were starving.

ODYSSEUS
You were slavering, like a dog.
You've wrecked everything.

EURYLOCHUS
I stand by my actions. You'll never get us home –
you've lost your bearings.

EURYBATES
Look – it moved.

POLITES
What did you say?

EURYBATES
The hide from that cow – I saw it . . .

POLITES
You have a fever.

ELPENOS
No – look. I saw it too. It's starting to . . . crawl.

EURYLOCHUS
Stop scaremongering – dead flesh doesn't move.

POLITES

You're wrong. Look, Eurylochus. That skull –
its jawbone opens and shuts.

ELPENOS

The eyes in the sockets roll and blink. Argh – the meat
on my plate.

POLITES

What?

ELPENOS

It's . . . twitching. It's alive. Urgh – get it off my leg.
Get it off.

EURYBATES

It's bewitched.

POLITES

What have we done, Eurylochus?
Every bone rattles and shakes, and the carcasses
squirm.

ELPENOS

I'm going to be sick.

EURYLOCHUS

It's nothing, it's just . . . we're imagining it.

ODYSSEUS

You've no notion of the chaos you've caused.

EURYLOCHUS

We're fine. It's the richness of the meat – making us
dream.

ODYSSEUS

You've no idea what demons you've released.

SHIPMATE (*from afar*)
Odysseus. The wind's changed.

POLITES
What did he say?

SHIPMATE
The wind's swung around. We should sail now, while it
blows fair.

POLITES
He's right. We should sail now, shouldn't we, Odysseus?

ODYSSEUS
Burn or bury what's left of those peaceful beasts.
Hide your shame in the sand.

ELPENOS
I'm not touching it – it's weird.

ODYSSEUS
You'll do as I say or you'll join it.
Then everyone onto the boat.

EURYLOCHUS
So the Cattle of the Sun writhe and wriggle after their
death –
so what? The wind changes in our favour.
The omens are good.

ODYSSEUS
The omens are BAD. The Gods are ANGRY.
And the doors of revenge open smoothly and quietly –
we're invited in, and into them we sail, their special
guests.

EURYLOCHUS
    I'm not afraid. We're no more than a few miles from
        home.

ODYSSEUS
    And just the small matter of eternity in between.
    I should leave you here.
    Eurylochus. Traitor. Slaughterman – killer of hope.

A thunderbolt splits the air.

IN THE PALACE OF THE PHAEACIANS

ODYSSEUS
No sooner do we cast off, no sooner do we
round the point, than black clouds slide over the sky,
gather over the boat like a solid black roof.
And Zeus, on behalf of the God of the Sun
whose precious cattle were cleaved apart,
triggered thunderbolt after thunderbolt.

It didn't take long. The end was quick. The mast
snapped like a twig. The hull fragmented,
every man was pitched into the churning swell –
I saw each face go past, gulping for breath,
reaching for a hand or rope. I saw heads
rise and sink, rise and sink, then rise no more.
Eurylochus was last, choking and thrashing,
eating the sea, breathing the sea till his lungs
were dead weights in his chest, pulling him down.

I saw every last shipmate and friend drown.

ALCINOUS
But you – you stand here before us – alive.
You lived to tell the tale.

ODYSSEUS
Lived, yes. And relive it now. As if I'm back there,
afloat in the sea with broken timbers and dead men.

I catch hold of a leather strap . . . it just comes to hand.
Why do I need it? I don't know but I
hold on. Hold on. The mast rolls past on its side . . . I
    mount it,

it throws me off . . . I scramble back on. And here's
a plank or spar . . . I lash the spar to the mast with
the strap . . . Now it's a floating cross . . . A crude raft.
   The
thump of the air . . . wind pummelling my back, landing
   punch
after punch . . . I won't let go . . . I dig my fingernails
into the wood . . . I breathe when the waves reload . . .
   Hold
my breath when they erupt . . . Then it's night
   suddenly . . .
I'm still alive. Still alive.

A current sweeps me along – a race of water, heading
   where . . .
backwards? Yes, back to the channel between rocks . . .
A cave on one side . . . on the other the water moans.
Scylla again, Charybdis again . . . Zeus – spare me – make
   it quick . . .
here comes an upswell . . . within reach – just – the limb
of a fig tree . . . I grab it . . . I'll hang on . . . The blood
   drains . . .
my arms are someone else's. Then . . . is it an hour I've . . .

is it an hour I've dangled over the vortex . . .
I'll die now. This moment I'll let go . . . Or this moment
now . . . or . . . Then an earth tremor, a quake under the
   sea . . .
All Charybdis swallows she vomits back again . . .
I let go, ride the rip curl, roll in the tidal wave . . .
and here's the puked-up remains of the raft . . .
I'll row with my hands . . . I'll row for four days, five
   days . . .

I'll row with my arms, six days, seven days, eight days,
   nine days, ten . . .

Delirious and breathless, Odysseus collapses on the floor.

ARETE
   Catch him, someone.

ALCINOUS
   Prop him in a chair – he's losing his balance.

ODYSSEUS
   No, I'm fine. Let me stand.

NAUSICAA
   Nonsense – you're only half conscious.
   Here's a drink, Odysseus. Not salt water now – just wine.

He drains the glass.

   Someone fill the glass again.

ODYSSEUS
   I'm fine, really.

ALCINOUS
   All so long ago, but still so clear in your mind.

ODYSSEUS
   A waking dream. A living nightmare.

   And you know the rest. I fetched up on Ogygia –
   Calypso's island. Seven years in her grip,
   then a tortuous journey here, then . . .

   Who knows, if your daughter hadn't taken pity on me,
   hadn't seen through the coat of leaves,
   and the lice-infested hair, and the filthy skin . . .
   hadn't see the man underneath. Who knows?
   Ten years at war. Ten years at sea.

ALCINOUS
    Odysseus, we . . .

ARETE
    No – let me.
    I was hesitant and unbelieving at first.
    You're a weaver of tales, Odysseus,
    And you're cunning and astute –
    the subject of your stories is your own cleverness.
    You've more guile than a million monkeys, I suspect.

    But there's no doubting your desire and intent.
    Your wife, your son, and your home –
    they're your magnetic north.
    Only a man with a passion and love like yours could have
        survived.

    There's no greater cause.
    Now I want nothing more than to see your journey
        complete.

ALCINOUS
    Believe me, Odysseus. When Queen Arete
    changes her mind, mountains have moved.
    Load a ship with treasure – gifts for our new friend –
    and sail him home at once.

NAUSICAA
    Must he leave now?

ARETE
    Yes, he must.

NAUSICAA
    But have him stay another week to gather his strength . . .

ARETE
Haven't you been listening?
Every step of the way something has tripped him up.
Opportunities have been traps.
Open doors have been prisons.
Invitations have been life sentences.

People have bedevilled him – not all of them men!

He won't be sidetracked again.
We won't offer the same temptation.

NAUSICAA
No, mother.

ODYSSEUS
So compassionate.
So . . . understanding.

ALCINOUS
Believe in us – we'll see you safe home.
We have the knack of these waters –
nothing will drive you back or knock you off course.

Is a boat prepared?

SERVANT
Ready and waiting.

ALCINOUS
With gifts on board?

SERVANT
Stacked to the limit, my lord.

ALCINOUS
What crew?

SERVANT
The best oarsmen from your fleet.

ODYSSEUS
My noble lord. Merciful queen. Gracious princess.

ALCINOUS
A toast. To Ithaca's returning King. To Odysseus.

ALL
TO ODYSSEUS.

HOMEWARD BOUND

SAILOR
The sun rising just as we near land. Perfect timing.

SKIPPER
And look – the morning star – a good sign.

SAILOR
Do you know this coast?

SKIPPER
I came here fishing once.

SAILOR
Where's the best place to land?

SKIPPER
Right here, pretty much, between these jutting
  promontories.
The ocean bed runs smoothly right up to the beach.
It's a natural harbour.

SAILOR
Will he be safe here?

SKIPPER
He's the king, isn't he? This is his land. Why should he
  fear?

SAILOR
Kings don't usually come home by the back door.
He might be mistaken for a spy or pirate and strung up.

SKIPPER
It's not our job to worry about these things.

Here we go. Punt on till we scrape the bottom,
then everyone out and drag it up the beach.

They haul the boat into the sand.

SKIPPER
OK. Well done. Where is he?

SAILOR
Asleep, look. Under this canvas.

SKIPPER
Don't wake him, then. You others, pile the treasure
out of reach of the sea.

SAILOR
Twenty years away from home – I wanted to see his face.

SKIPPER
No, let him rest.

SAILOR
What's the longest you've ever been away for?

SKIPPER
Twelve weeks. Felt like for ever.

SAILOR
So what must this be like?
I bet even his own dog won't remember him.

SKIPPER
I can't think that a man like this will have been forgotten.

SAILOR
The world turns. Fashions change. People move on.

SKIPPER
   Some things are worth waiting for.

SAILOR
   No one would wait that long for me.

SKIPPER
   We'll bear him on this pallet
   and set him down on the beach.

They lift Odysseus from the boat and leave him sleeping on the shore.

SAILOR
   Sure we shouldn't wake him?

SKIPPER
   No. This seems right.
   Throw the canvas back over his shoulders.

SAILOR
   It'll be like waking up from a coma.
   Like coming back from the dead.

SKIPPER
   All unloaded?
   One big shove then to cast off.

   Good luck, tired Odysseus. Sleeping King of Ithaca.
   Welcome home.

III

IN THE PALACE OF ODYSSEUS

The suitors are gambling and feasting.

EURYMACHUS
> You bet three. I bet five, and another five.

AMPHINOMUS
> That's thirteen.

EURYMACHUS
> You're a mathematical genius!
> Hey – more wine over here. And more meat.

AMPHINOMUS
> Takes the fun out of it, doesn't it?

EURYMACHUS
> The fun out of what?

AMPHINOMUS
> Gambling. We drink like princes and we eat like kings.
> Whatever we shout for arrives on a silver plate.
> I've put on weight.

EURYMACHUS
> I never get tired of winning or sick of losing.
> Now lay your money down and roll the stones.

They roll the pebbles across the table.

> Ha! Pay up. You're a born loser, Amphinomus,
> I don't know why I hang about with you – it might rub
>   off.

AMPHINOMUS
> You've done all right by me.

EURYMACHUS
   True – it keeps my purse fat. But look, there goes the
      biggest prize.

AMPHINOMUS
   Where?

*The hall goes quiet as the suitors register Penelope's
presence.*

EURYMACHUS
   On the balcony – same time every night.
   (*shouts*)
   My sovereign lady. Won't you join us for a drink?

   Or a bite to eat?

   There's more than enough. Look at this plump game bird,
   freshly roasted. Won't you share a leg with me, my lady?

   Or a breast? Will you share a breast?

AMPHINOMUS
   Leave her alone.

EURYMACHUS
   Shall we prise open the wishbone together, my lady?
   Part it wide and make a wish.

Laughter in the hall.

AMPHINOMUS
   You're deplorable.

EURYMACHUS
   What's rattled your cage?

AMPHINOMUS
   I just think we should show her some respect.
   Vulgarity – it's hardly the way to her heart.

EURYMACHUS
  And how much respect has she showed us,
  stringing us along all these years? She's the vulgar one.

AMPHINOMUS
  It's not what I call courtship.

EURYMACHUS
  She's in no position to pick and choose.
  She's a widow in all but name, and before long
  she'll be penniless, and those looks won't last for ever.
  Pretty soon she'll be happy to marry a goat-herd.
  So stop flapping. We're in the box seat.

AMPHINOMUS
  If Odysseus ever comes back . . .

EURYMACHUS
  Well, he isn't coming back, so stop mithering.

Penelope leaves the balcony and a door closes behind her.

EURYMACHUS
  Now look what you've done – you've scared her off.
  Get your money out – we'll double the stakes.
  Anyone else for a game?

Antinous strides into the hall.

ANTINOUS
  Put those away.

EURYMACHUS
  Hey – I'm in the middle of a winning streak.

ANTINOUS
  Your luck just changed. Crowd around and listen.
  News just reached me. Telemachus is back on Ithaca.

EURYMACHUS
    What? We had men on the cliffs and in the bay.

ANTINOUS
    He slipped past.

EURYMACHUS
    How can a man slip past a hundred spears and knives?
    A sea-snake couldn't have wriggled through that lot
        unscathed.

ANTINOUS
    Well, he did. He was seen in the hills.

EURYMACHUS
    Useless. A bunch of hopeless bunglers.
    I should have done it myself.

AMPHINOMUS
    This is a bad omen.

ANTINOUS
    Let's keep superstition out of it. Although . . .
    it's true. The fingerprints of the Gods are all over this.
    Those watchmen kept guard all around the clock,
    right across the bay. It was a wall of steel.
    Only a God or Goddess could have spirited that boy home.

AMPHINOMUS
    Not a boy any more, then.

EURYMACHUS
    He's a lickspittle. A beardless wonder.

ANTINOUS
    No, Amphinomus is right.
    By stealing back to Ithaca he's proved what some of us
        feared –

that he's crafty and determined.
He's his father's son, in other words.
And now he's roaming the island,
turning people against us, murmuring in their ears.
We've no alternative.

AMPHINOMUS

What – murder him in cold blood?

ANTINOUS

You didn't hesitate before,
when we meant to finish him off at sea.

AMPHINOMUS

Out of sight, out of mind. But he's the heir to the
    kingdom –
we can't hunt him down in his own land.

EURYMACHUS

Kill him now.

ANTINOUS

Agreed. This thing needs bringing to a head.
Then we'll offer gifts to his mother –
she'll choose the man who makes the best offer . . .

EURYMACHUS

And we'll all live happily ever after.

AMPHINOMUS

I say we should consult the Gods – seek their judgement.

ANTINOUS

They've made their move by bringing Telemachus home.
They mean to test us – see how we respond.

We won't disappoint them.

OLYMPUS

ATHENA

Zeus? Father?

ZEUS

I'm resting.

ATHENA

It won't exhaust you to turn your head.
Look down through the clouds. What do you see?

ZEUS

Nothing. It's misty.

ATHENA

Wait a moment.
(*She blows the clouds apart.*)
Now what do you see? There, where I'm pointing.

ZEUS

An island.

ATHENA

Not just any island. Ithaca.

ZEUS

Has Athena taken to giving mighty Zeus lessons in
geography?

ATHENA

Look at that beach on the west coast.
That cove, between the two headlands.
Notice anything on the strand-line?

ZEUS

    Driftwood?

ATHENA

    Of a kind.

ZEUS

    No, it's something alive. A large squid, is it? A dolphin?

ATHENA

    It's a man.

ZEUS

    Ah, and not just any man, I presume?

ATHENA

    Look at the hands, the hair, the limbs beneath the clothes.
    Odysseus, home after twenty years.

ZEUS

    And now he sleeps like a foetus,
    curled in a ball with his face buried in his chest.
    Let's see if a few drops of rain might bring him round.

ATHENA

    No, don't wake him.

ZEUS

    Very well. The beautiful irony isn't lost on me.
    The suffering hero arrives home in slumbering innocence.

ATHENA

    But is he home for good, or does Poseidon
    still chase him for his pound of flesh?

ZEUS

    Who can say, in the great scheme of things?
    Who can predict what might happen next?

Besides, your man, Odysseus –
he might be sleeping like a baby in the womb
but he rears up like a cobra when he's roused.
He blinded the Cyclops with a burning lance –
Poseidon's son! My nephew. Poseidon has a case.

ATHENA

He's your brother. Call him off.

ZEUS

I can't do that.

ATHENE

Then I'll go to Odysseus. I'll intervene.

ZEUS

Athena, not so fast.

ATHENA

He's served his time. I won't have him
clawed back into the sea by some freak wave.

ZEUS

You're being hasty – you're acting irrationally – like one
of them.

ATHENA

I'll guide him safely inland.

ZEUS

Well, if you must you must. At least go in disguise.

ATHENA

I'll appear as a shepherd boy. Goodbye, father.

ZEUS

Goodbye, goodbye, goodbye.

She's right. Poor wretch of a man –
twenty years an exile – enough is enough.
Odysseus will be spared.
But Poseidon bears his grudge like a birthright –
he'll have to be bought off.

So those Phaeacian oarsmen, who carried him
over the waves, whose craft still skims the surface
of Poseidon's watery fields . . . who can say? Who can
   say?

ON THE BEACH AT ITHACA

*A violent wave crashes in the distance as Poseidon wrecks
the Phaeacian ship. The echo of it carries across the water,
waking Odysseus from his sleep.*

ODYSSEUS
    What . . . a dream . . . the end of the world . . .
    No, only a storm at sea.
    A freak wave cracking the keel of some poor sailing ship.
    Snapping it like a twig. Just the Gods doing their thing.

He stands and dusts himself down.

    How long did I sleep? Too long. And too deep –
    those sweet-talking Phaeacians. The moment
    I closed my eyes they dumped me on the nearest beach.

    Did they take away their gifts as well,
    giving to me with the right hand,
    taking back with the left?
    I bet they couldn't keep their fingers off this stash of loot.

He lays his hands on the riches, piled on the beach.

    No, all here.
    But what's the use of a golden brooch
    or a ruby ring or a crown studded with precious stones
    in a God-forsaken land. I'm discarded. A castaway.
    I'm the king of nothing and nowhere again.
    (*shouts into the air*)
    I'M THE KING OF OBLIVION.

ATHENA (*disguised as a shepherd boy*)
    You seem troubled, stranger. Are you lost?

ODYSSEUS (*surprised and flustered*)
Er . . . lost . . . yes. Shipwrecked. Thrown onto the beach.
Lost and a little bit delirious.

ATHENA
But the sea's been calm for weeks.

ODYSSEUS
It happened . . . some time and distance away. I drifted.

ATHENA
Lucky to be alive, then?

ODYSSEUS
Lucky beyond all imagining.
But my thoughts are in a mess – all my senses are fuddled.
The wind's whistled in my ear, the sun's warmed my
    brain
and salt water has fouled my blood.
The workings of my mind are out of kilter with the world.
I'm completely lost. I have to ask you – what island is
    this?

ATHENA
You mean you don't know?

ODYSSEUS
Hand on heart – I've no idea.

ATHENA
Then you're in worse shape than you think.

Don't you recognize this famous place,
with its rocky outcrops and jutting crags?
It's not huge, but it's rich in woodland
and birdlife, and the wells never run dry,
and crops and vines thrive in its deep soil,

and goats and cattle are fat with milk,
and herbs season the air . . .

ODYSSEUS
No, I . . .

ATHENA
Breathe its smell – doesn't it strike home?

ODYSSEUS (*breathing in*)
I must admit there's something . . .

ATHENA
Say its name. Ithaca! It's famous everywhere –
even in Troy, and that's a world away. Say it.

ODYSSEUS (*astonished*)
Ithaca?

ATHENA
Don't say you haven't heard of it.

ODYSSEUS
Ithaca. Ithaca? I . . .
(*concealing his feelings*)
I mean – yes, I've come across that name.

You see, I'm a sailor from Crete. With children
waiting for me, children with mouths to feed.
This pile of treasure, it's mainly for them.
I was sailing west when . . .

ATHENA
Odysseus – you're cunning and wily, right to the last,
some might go as far as to call you sly.
But you can stop your twisting and turning now.
You're no more a sailor from Crete than I'm a shepherd
   boy.

ODYSSEUS

Who are you? What do you want?

ATHENA

Pallas Athena. Daughter of Zeus.

ODYSSEUS

My Goddess.

ATHENA

I've followed your fortunes, Odysseus.
Stood like a shield in front of you
or at your shoulder in silence.

ODYSSEUS

I've felt your presence. You've been my lucky talisman.

ATHENA

No, much more.
I've been your pole star, and your armour plating.
Without me, you wouldn't have made it this far.
You wouldn't have lived.

ODYSSEUS

I can't take it in.
I daren't let myself believe.

ATHENA

Believe it, Odysseus. You're home.

ODYSSEUS

My eyes begin to recognize the signs –
those stones . . . those plants . . . the birds . . . even the
    clouds –
all images of Ithaca – all native to this land.
But my heart won't let it be true.

ATHENA

    It's as true as the ground you kneel on.
    Feel the sand. Pick it up. It's Ithaca – every last grain.

ODYSSEUS (*astonished*)

    Ithaca – right here in my hand.

ATHENA

    Which doesn't mean your journey's over.
    Hordes of suitors are camped in your house,
    loving the day your wife declares herself a widow –
    your death would open the bedroom doors for one of
       those hyenas.
    And Penelope, who waits and waits,
    you can't just go striding home after so long . . .

ODYSSEUS

    I know. I need to prove myself to her.
    She needs . . .
    We need to prove ourselves to ourselves –
    husband to wife.

ATHENA

    Never impulsive. Clever like a cat.
    Look, I'll bring down the mist – slip through its curtain.
    Go and find Eumaeus, your old swineherd.

ODYSSEUS

    What are you doing?

ATHENA

    Odysseus wouldn't make it within a mile of his palace –
    the suitors have their spies and their assassins.
    But an old man,
    with shrunken skin,
    sagging limbs,

a head of silvery hair
and two dull stones in his eyes . . .

She transforms him into an old man.

ODYSSEUS
  It's hardly how I imagined my return.
  Tottering home, a wizened beggar.

ATHENA
  There'll be no grand entrance.
  Less self-consciousness and more self-preservation –
  that's what's needed on this occasion.

ODYSSEUS
  What about my son, Telemachus? Tell me about my son.

ATHENA
  Follow the path to the right of the cliffs.
  (*Her voice trails off into the distance.*)
  Go now before the fog catches you in its net.

ODYSSEUS
  Athena, wait . . .

  A nightmare twenty years in the wilds of the world.
  Then I open my eyes and I'm home. I wake from sleep,
  and I'm home.

THE LOYAL SWINEHERD

Odysseus approaches Eumaeus' farmstead. Dogs bark as he opens the gate and nears the door.

EUMAEUS (*from inside*)
Who's there? Who's trespassing on my land?

ODYSSEUS
A shipwrecked sailor, from Crete.
The tide washed me up on your shore.
I'm a friendly stranger. I don't mean any harm.

EUMAEUS (*opening the door*)
Friendly, eh? Oh, yes, there's no doubt about that.

ODYSSEUS (*thinking he may have been recognized*)
But you've never seen me before. How can you tell?

EUMAEUS
I can't, but these hounds can.
They've got a keen nose for that kind of thing.
They can smell danger from twenty fields away.
If you'd been a trouble-maker, old timer,
you'd be dog-meat by now.

ODYSSEUS
Then praise to all animals and their sense of right and
wrong.

EUMAEUS
I'm a farmer – I praise animals every day.
Well, come inside. It's no stately home but it's warm and
dry.

They go inside the hut.

EUMAEUS

Take the seat by the fire.

ODYSSEUS

Isn't that your seat?

EUMAEUS

Visitors have pride of place in this house.
This whole island's famous for its hospitality.
Better it wasn't – that's what I sometimes think.

ODYSSEUS

What can you mean by that?

EUMAEUS

Down at the palace.
It's crawling with spongers and layabouts,
dozens of them out-staying their welcome.
Scavengers they are. Dingoes.

ODYSSEUS

The head of the house must be a generous man.

EUMAEUS

The most generous I've ever known, and the wisest.
Odysseus – do you know of him?

ODYSSEUS

Er . . . I've heard his name, of course.

EUMEAUS

A true king. And with vast wealth –
land, cattle, crops, an army, a sailing fleet . . .

But he's missing, presumed dead.
Twenty years in his absence I've tended his flocks
while the household's gone to rack and ruin.

ODYSSEUS
    Does he have family? A widow, perhaps.

EUMAEUS
    Penelope – loyal as the moon to the earth.
    But she can't hold out much longer.
    Keeping those suitors at bay – it's like holding back a
        flood.

ODYSSEUS
    No children to take up his role?

EUMAEUS
    A fine son, Telemachus. He's abroad
    in search of his father – or his father's grave.
    There's a rumour he's back on the island,
    but that's hope talking. Here, have a bowl of stew.

ODYSSEUS
    You're a kind man. You offer me shelter and food
    without even asking my name.

EUMAEUS
    I can see who you are.

ODYSSEUS
    You can?

EUMAEUS
    You're a working man like me.
    You've got a sun-beaten face and leather hands
    and enough dirt under your finger nails to plant corn in.
    You're old – older than me even!
    You've lived a hard life under the stars – right?

ODYSSEUS
    Right.

EUMAEUS

We're two of a kind then. What else is there to know?
How's the stew?

ODYSSEUS

Everything I need. Bless you.

Outside, the dogs are excited.

Sounds like another stranger coming to your door.

EUMAEUS

More like a friend, I'd say, listening to those dogs –
sounds like they're kissing his feet!
Another herdsmen from over the hill, I'd guess.

There is a knock at the door.

Come in. Always room for one more.

Telemachus opens the door and stands in the door frame.

(*delirious with excitement*)
Telemachus Telemachus Telemachus!

TELEMACHUS

Eumaeus – loyal and trusted friend.

EUMAEUS

Telemachus Telemachus Telemachus!
Give thanks to the Gods and planets.
Telemachus Telemachus Telemachus!
Give thanks to a thousand stars.
Ho! Telemachus – wasn't I just singing his praises?

ODYSSEUS

To the sky.

TELEMACHUS
    Who's the old man?

EUMAEUS
    A wanderer – hungry and out of breath.
    Telemachus Telemachus Telemachus!
    A miracle – I'd only a minute ago spoken your name!
    Tell him, hadn't I just this second spoken his name?

ODYSSEUS
    Not more than a moment since.

EUMAEUS
    Tell me all about your trip. But first
    this calls for a slap-up feast!
    I'll skewer the juiciest pig in the pen.
    Crank up the fire while I'm outside.

    Oh, it's good to see you, young man.
    Telemachus Telemachus Telemachus . . .
    Ha!

He goes outside, chuckling to himself.

TELEMACHUS
    Well, I haven't seen happiness like that for a long while.

ODYSSEUS
    You've put him in high spirits. He adores you.

TELEMACHUS
    It's inherited glory. He adores my father more.

ODYSSEUS
    Your father?

TELEMACHUS
    Odysseus.

ODYSSEUS

  Of course. Any news of him on your travels?

TELEMACHUS

  Rumours. Gossip. Nothing solid.
  I've told myself I might never see him again.
  I'm prepared for the worst.

ODYSSEUS

  Would you know him if he returned?

TELEMACHUS

  I was only a baby when he left.
  But they say he stands out. They say he's a man
  above and beyond ordinary men, and unmistakable.

ODYSSEUS

  You must . . . miss him.

TELEMACHUS

  It hurts. A physical pain.

ODYSSEUS

  He must miss you too, a fine son.

TELEMACHUS (*upset*)

  If his heart still beats in his chest.

ODYSSEUS

  I apologize. I'm only an old stranger. I've overstepped the
    mark.

TELEMACHUS

  Your words weren't meant to harm, though.
  You have a kindness that shines through.
  I'll . . . help Eumaeus catch his pig.

Telemachus leaves the hut.

ODYSSEUS (*to himself, his voice full of emotion*)
My son, my living flesh. My miraculous son.

Athena appears from nowhere.

ATHENA
Do you hear me, Odysseus?

ODYSSEUS
Voices in the air?
No, I can't make out . . . who is it, standing in the dark
    corner?
Show your face.

ATHENA
Don't you recognize your lucky Goddess, your guiding
    light?

ODYSSEUS
Athena – what if they see you?
You gave me this disguise – now you'll blow my cover.

ATHENA
It's time your son knows you for who you are.
Then the two of you can hatch a plan –
you'll know what to say, I've planted the seed in your
    head.
Time's running down.

Here – I fling magic at you.
I throw you back the strength in your bones,
and the colour in your hair,
and the smoothness of your skin,
the straightness in your spine,
your supple limbs,

and here – here's fire for your eyes,
and a worthy shirt for your shoulders.

Who wouldn't recognize you now, handsome Odysseus?

ODYSSEUS
One minute I'm a dull old man,
the next I'm shining like a king.
What will my son say?

ATHENA
Make the most of your appearance – it's just a fleeting
    glimpse.
Here comes Telemachus. I'll dissolve into air again.

Telemachus returns to the hut.

TELEMACHUS
There's a comical sight.
Those grunters are like greased lightning, and . . .

What's happening here? Your skin, your face . . .

ODYSSEUS
Don't be afraid, Telemachus.

TELEMACHUS
This is freakish. Supernatural.

ODYSSEUS
I'm the same person.

TELEMACHUS
No, you were a mortal – an old, withered man.
Now – you glow. Like . . . like a God.

ODYSSEUS
I'm no God – just a man transformed by the touch of a
  Goddess.
Look at me, Telemachus.
Who am I?

TELEMACHUS
You're a trickster. You'll put a spell on me.

ODYSSEUS
It's no trick. Look at me.
Who am I?

TELEMACHUS
You deceive me.

ODYSSEUS
LOOK AT ME. Look at me, Telemachus, my son.

TELEMACHUS
. . . Your son?

ODYSSEUS
What did you say, that Odysseus is unmistakable?
Then don't mistake him. Recognize him at once.

TELEMACHUS (*stunned*)
That's what they say. What I've always been told.

ODYSSEUS
See me for who I am. You'll see no other Odysseus.

I hold out a father's hand to you, Telemachus.
Take it. Take it, Telemachus.

Let the bond be remade. Let this family begin again.

TELEMACHUS
Father? Father?

Telemachus breaks down in tears in front of his father.

ODYSSEUS
Weep with me, my son. Weep with me.

Then swear an oath – to keep my return a secret.

TELEMACHUS
Father. My father.

ODYSSEUS
Swear an oath, Telemachus,
there's a bloody feud to be won.

TELEMACHUS
But the two of us can't settle it alone.
Forty or fifty men sprawl in our home.
I need to use your name to recruit an armed force.

ODYSSEUS
Swear!
An absolute oath – a bond between father and son.
Go to the palace but tell no one – not even Penelope
    herself.
I'll appear as a beggar again –
if I'm insulted and abused just bite your lip.
Play along with the deceit.

TELEMACHUS
Twenty years you've been out of our lives.
Now I've got to pretend you don't exist.

ODYSSEUS
Swear an oath, Telemachus – everything depends on it.

TELEMACHUS
  I swear.

ODYSSEUS
  Save whatever you're feeling – anger, bitterness,
     impatience . . .
  I'll give the signal when the time comes.
  Then pick up a spear and a sword and stand beside me,
  and let rip.

OLYMPUS

ATHENA
Father?

ZEUS
Yes, indeed. I was watching. Really very touching.

ATHENA
You scoff at my intervention!

ZEUS (*genuinely moved*)
Not at all – I mean every word of it.
The love between a parent and child – it's . . . a rarity.
Without condition. Uncompromised. A kind of purity.
And mortals – they have their shortcomings, millions of
   them,
but they show their feelings.
And when they do . . .

Come here, child, let me hold you.

ATHENA (*embarrassed*)
Father.

ZEUS (*somewhat rejected*)
Yes, you're right. Outward displays of affection. Frowned
   upon.

ATHENA
No, I didn't mean to . . .

ZEUS (*becoming Godlike again*)
Frowned upon, I said.
In any case, your work there isn't finished.
Unless it's just some hobby you've tired of?

ATHENA

    I'll see it through right to the finish.
    I'll stand at his shoulder to the very end.

ZEUS

    To intervene when insult and indignity come his way?

ATHENA

    Exactly right.

ZEUS

    Exactly wrong.

ATHENA

    But father . . .

ZEUS

    Take advice from someone who knows about retribution
       and revenge.

    Let his flesh soak up as much bitterness as it can take.
    Let his nerves come close to overloading with pain.
    Let him stare into the dark, let him brush with terror,
    stand eyelash to eyelash with fear.

ATHENA

    How much more can he stomach?

ZEUS

    As much as it takes. Then he'll turn it to rage.
    He'll need all the fury he can summon.
    Anything short of total agony, utter hurt, and he'll fall
       short.

    Let him suffer first, or he'll fail.
    Let the sound of his wife's sadness eat into his heart.

PENELOPE'S BED-CHAMBER

PENELOPE
And bring them home safe.
Land them safe in Ithaca.
My husband and my son.
Gods of the heavens, I beg of you.

EURYCLEIA (*entering the room*)
Sorry, ma'am, I didn't mean to interrupt your prayers.

PENELOPE
No, I was talking to myself.

EURYCLEIA
I can come back.

PENELOPE
Stay and freshen the room with flowers. I need some air.

Penelope goes out onto the balcony. Below her, the suitors are plotting.

ANTINOUS
Any sign of the son yet?

EURYMACHUS
Neither hide nor hair. We've got prying eyes
all over the island, but they've seen nothing.

AMPHINOMUS
He's getting help from above – that's my theory.

ANTINOUS
He'll need it if any of my men catch him.

PENELOPE (*to herself*)
  Bloodsuckers. Merciless, heartless creatures.

AMPHINOMUS
  What if he turns up here?

ANTINOUS
  What if he does?

AMPHINOMUS
  We can't run him through with a spear on his own doorstep.

ANTINOUS
  You're a flaky one.

AMPHINOMUS
  I want this matter resolved as much as anyone,
  But to cut him down in front of his mother . . .

EURYMACHUS
  I'll quite happily tear him organ from organ.

PENELOPE (*unable to contain her anger*)
  You VIOLATE me.

The suitors are shocked into silence.

  You, Amphinomus – I thought better of you.

AMPHINOMUS
  My lady, I . . .

PENELOPE
  Eurymachus – your parents raised a brute.
  And you, Antinous – you're inhuman
  and sadistic – right down to your roots.
  They say you're the finest young man
  on the island – what must the worst be like?

Your father came here once, on the run.
He'd fallen in with a bad lot. Angry mobs
wanted him strung up from a post,
but Odysseus took him in, harboured him,
helped him ride out the storm.
Now you trash the house of Odysseus,
and drool over his grieving wife,
and make plans to butcher his son.
(*tearful*)
You're monsters. You're breaking my heart.
Do you understand? Get out of this house.
Get out. GET OUT. GET OUT.

*Penelope rushes back into her room, slams the door and
collapses on the bed in tears.*

EURYCLEIA
  My lady! My lady!

PENELOPE
  Leave me.

EURYCLEIA
  But my lady . . .

PENELOPE
  Leave me – do you hear?

EURYCLEIA
  As you wish, my lady.
  Except, if you'd only turn you head this way,
  let your eyes do some seeing instead of all these
    waterworks.

PENELOPE
  How dare you. Leave me alone with my tears.

TELEMACHUS (*gently*)
    Mother.

Penelope bites back her tears to listen again for the voice.

    Mother.

PENELOPE
    Telemachus.

EURYCLEIA (*giddy*)
    I bumped into him walking up the back steps.
    Up the back steps!
    I kissed his face and his hands like he was my own!
    Look at him – I threw myself into his arms!

PENELOPE
    Leave us, Eurycleia.

EURYCLEIA
    Well, I only . . . In the circumstances . . . Yes, my lady.

    Threw myself into his arms I did . . .
    Up the back stairs indeed . . .

She leaves the room.

PENELOPE
    You sneak home as secretly as you left.

TELEMACHUS
    Is that the welcome I get?

PENELOPE
    You stole away with no word of where you were going or
        why.
    Against my will.
    You left me here on my own.

TELEMACHUS
  Inaction was killing me.
  I had to go in search of news of my father –
  your husband, Odysseus.

PENELOPE
  So spit it out. Is he dead?

TELEMACHUS (*mumbling*)
  No hard news.
  A story that said he was trapped by the nymph
    Calypso . . .

PENELOPE
  Held in another woman's arms?

TELEMACHUS
  Held there by force.
  And rumours of battles and skirmishes on the way home
    from Troy . . .

PENELOPE
  Don't think I'm a stone.
  Don't think my heart didn't fly up when I heard your
    voice.
  They were plotting to kill you –
  I thought you'd walked straight onto their spears.

TELEMACHUS
  I'm no longer a child, mother.

PENELOPE
  Then give me news of your father.

TELEMACHUS
  I have nothing to tell. I . . . can't say.

PENELOPE
So leave me to grieve. Nothing has changed.
I'll wind myself in this shroud of bedsheets again.

TELEMACHUS
Don't languish.
Wash with water instead of tears.
Put on clean robes, go to the roof and pray to Zeus.

I have business to attend to.
Be glad that I'm alive.

Laughter and cheering comes from the hall below.
Telemachus leaves the room and addresses the suitors from
the balcony.

Up here. No, not a ghost.
Not dead – sorry to disappoint you.
Still got your heads in the trough, I see?
Well, eat up, eat up.
We're famed for our hospitality,
we won't turn anyone away.
We won't give you the satisfaction.

Cooks – more meat on the spit.
Carver – double each portion – good thick slices.
Waiters – be quicker with the plates.
You with the jar of wine – don't stint,
charge every glass to the brink.
Slake them to the last drop.
Feed them to the last grain.

Penelope can hear Telemachus' words from her chamber.

PENELOPE (*to herself*)
Odysseus – come home. Come home for your wife and
    son.

ARGOS

Athena has restored Odysseus' disguise. Still believing him to be a shipwrecked sailor from Crete, Eumaeus is escorting him towards the royal palace.

EUMAEUS
 All right there, old timer?

ODYSSEUS
 I'm just about managing, thanks.

EUMAEUS
 Not going too fast, am I? I'm no spring chicken myself
 but you've got a good number of years over me.

ODYSSEUS
 There's a few miles left in these old legs yet.

EUMAEUS
 What about Telemachus, eh?
 See – he doesn't know you from a hole in the road,
 but he only invites you down to his palace for a square
   meal –
 and you a perfect stranger, and hardly royalty – no
   offence and all that.
 He's a fine boy grown into a fine man.

ODYSSEUS
 His father would be proud of him.

EUMAEUS
 His heart would burst – believe me.
 That's one reunion I hope to live to see.

Melanthius, another herder, crosses their path.

MELANTHIUS
Well, look who it isn't.

EUMAEUS (*to Odysseus*)
Ignore him. He's no better than me.

MELANTHIUS
Eumaeus, loyal swineherd to Odysseus.
So who's the clapped-out old creature you're taking to
   market today?

EUMAEUS
I'll not trade insults with you, Melanthius. Good day.

MELANTHIUS
I thought you were the creakiest pile of bones on the
   whole island,
but this one takes the biscuit.
What a filth-bag.

EUMAEUS
Good day, Melanthius.

MELANTHIUS
Hey, beggar-man thing – are you dead or alive?

EUMAEUS
We're minding our own business, why don't you mind
   yours?

MELANTHIUS
It is my business.
There's too many spongers and cadgers hanging around
without you towing one more into town.
If he comes to my house begging for scraps and crusts

he'll get a boot in the face,
then I'll slam his pilfering fingers in the door.
(*He hits Odysseus with his stick.*)
There's something for your troubles, you scum.
Get back to your shanty.

EUMAEUS
Leave him alone!

MELANTHIUS
Oh, do you want some too?

EUMAEUS
We're heading for the palace, if you must know.

MELANTHIUS
The palace! Those suitors will rip him to pieces just for
    sport.
They'll break stools over his head,
they'll use his teeth for dice.

EUMAEUS (*to Odysseus*)
Take no heed. Just let it go.

MELANTHIUS (*his voice disappearing behind them*)
The palace – oh that's a good one.
They'll use his backside for target practice.
They'll push a hook up his arse and pull him inside
    out . . .

EUMAEUS
No respect. No consideration. It never used to be like this.

A dog barks and whines pitifully.

Well, would you look at that sad sight,
a sign of the times if ever there was one.

ODYSSEUS

What's a noble breed of dog like that doing sleeping on a
pile of dung?

EUMAEUS

You might well ask. That's Argos. Odysseus' dog.

ODYSSEUS

Argos?

EUMAEUS

Trained him as a pup, he did. Taught him to hunt.
But then he sailed for Troy – never saw him quarter a field
or bring down a hare going at full lick.
I swear he was the best hound ever. Now look at him.

ODYSSEUS

Come here, boy.

EUMAEUS

Jumping with fleas and ticks.

ODYSSEUS

There's a boy. There's a boy.

EUMAEUS

Eyes all gummed up, ears weeping from bites and cuts.

ODYSSEUS

You're a beautiful feller. There's a boy.

EUMAEUS

Gone in the legs. Horrible to watch. Well, he likes you
right enough.

ODYSSEUS

There now, rest your head, old boy. There now. There
now.

EUMAEUS

He's a tired one. Poor thing can hardly stand.
Likes the taste of your hand though. Must be the salt.

ODYSSEUS

Lie down, lie down. There's a boy. Lie down.
You sleep. It's over now. Lie down. You sleep. There's a
boy.

The dog stops breathing.

EUMAEUS

Is he gone?

ODYSSEUS

He's at rest now.

EUMAEUS

It's a blessing.
Only had eyes for his master.

You've got a gentle way with animals, old timer, I'll say
that.

ODYSSEUS (*whispering*)

Sleep now, Argos. Loyal friend.

Music and laughter drifts towards them from the palace.

Someone's having a good time.

EUMAEUS

The Palace of Odysseus. Magnificent, eh?

ODYSSEUS

Like a mirage.

EUMAEUS

Not as splendid as it was

before those mongrels made themselves at home, but still
   a fine spectacle.
Imagine coming home – seeing that after twenty years at
   war and at sea.
Imagine a feeling like that.

ODYSSEUS
   Yes, imagine.

EUMAEUS
   Well, come on, the main door's standing open. Don't
   dawdle.

ODYSSEUS ENTERS HIS PALACE

EUMAEUS
Take a seat, old feller. Look, there's noble Telemachus,
still doing his duty, hosting this pack of free-loaders.

ODYSSEUS
Shall I approach him myself?

EUMAEUS
Why not – he invited you here. He won't have forgotten.

Odysseus approaches Telemachus.

TELEMACHUS (*hushed*)
Father.

ODYSSEUS (*whispering*)
Don't let them see through our pretence. Act accordingly.
I need to test these suitors man by man – but how?

TELEMACHUS
Here – take this bowl around. Beg from them one by one.
You'll get the measure of them by their response.

Odysseus takes a bowl and approaches the suitors in turn.

ODYSSEUS (*to Amphinomus*)
Any crusts to spare, young man, sir? Anything going
begging?

AMPHINOMUS
Who's this, then?

ODYSSEUS
Just an old man with a grumbling belly.

AMPHINOMUS
>Here, take these ribs – you can dig the marrow from
>them. Now shoo.

ODYSSEUS
>Very kind, my young sir. God bless you.

He approaches Eurymachus.

>Sir, if you'll beg my pardon.
>Can you spare a scrap or two from your plate?

EURYMACHUS
>What – fuck off – I'm eating. Whatever happened to good
>manners?

ODYSSEUS
>I'm ashamed to be asking. Don't make it worse for me,
>sir.
>Just a crust or a half-chewed bone or a burnt sausage.
>My belly thinks my throat's been cut.

EURYMACHUS
>It might come true.
>You're a scavenger, whoever you are, and a filthy one at
>that.
>Well, it's worth a lump of gristle just to keep you away.
>There – on the floor – where the dogs eat. Now vanish.

Odysseus approaches Antinous.

ODYSSEUS
>Fine young sir, if I could trouble you . . .

ANTINOUS
>Look what the wind blew in.

ODYSSEUS

If you could spare a morsel of meat for a man in his later
years.

ANTINOUS

Did someone leave the gates of the graveyard open?

The suitors laugh.

ODYSSEUS

I apologize if my appearance offends you.

ANTINOUS

Appearance? It's your existence I object to.
Now stop breathing on me and crawl back in your hole.

AMPHINOMUS

Don't be ruthless, Antinous. It's only human to be hungry.

ANTINOUS

This swamp donkey isn't human. Who let him in?

EUMAEUS

He came with me.

EURYMACHUS

And who are you?

EUMAEUS

Eumaeus, loyal herdsman to Odysseus.

ANTINOUS

A pig-man – that figures! One swine leading another.

ODYSSEUS

Just a bite, sir. That kidney on your plate – you wouldn't
miss it.

ANTINOUS (*flaring with anger*)
You ignorant, shameless scrounger.
Get your loathsome hand away from my meal.
Pig-man, don't you think there are enough mouths to feed
without bringing beggars into the hall?

EUMAEUS
Aye, and you're one of them yourself. What's the
    difference?
You and your lot – you're a swarm of locusts.

ANTINOUS
You impertinent wretch.

TELEMACHUS
Ignore him, Eumaeus. Don't waste your breath.

EUMAEUS
He's got some neck, though. Him and his friends
leaching the blood from this proud house,
then he turns round and tells another man not to beg.
    Outrageous!

ODYSSEUS
Even the shell from your egg, sir.
The cow's horn, the billy goat's beard – anything.

ANTINOUS
You're right. You're so right. Where are my manners?
Here, take a seat. This stool I'm sitting on – you can have
    it.
(*He smashes the stool over Odysseus' head.*)
Right across your skull.

AMPHINOMUS
Antinous, for God's sake calm down.

[234]

EURYMACHUS
    Keep out of it. Let him have his say.

AMPHINOMUS
    It's an offence in the eyes of the Gods to mistreat a
        stranger.

EURYMACHUS
    The Gods don't care about him.
    If they did, he wouldn't be a good-for-nothing beggar.

TELEMACHUS (*under his breath, attending to Odysseus*)
    Father, are you hurt?

ODYSSEUS
    Ignore it.

TELEMACHUS
    I won't stand for this any longer. I'll kill Antinous right
        now.

ODYSSEUS
    If you want what's best for us you'll swallow your pride.
    Now get away from me.
    (*hisses*)
    Get away.

ANTINOUS
    Fetch me another seat, somebody.
    And throw that flea-ridden dosser into the street.

PENELOPE (*from the balcony*)
    As long as this is the house of Odysseus I'll say how
        guests are treated.

ODYSSEUS (*hushed, captivated by the first sight of his wife*)
    Penelope.

TELEMACHUS (*hushed, to Odysseus*)
Now it's your turn to hold your tongue.

PENELOPE
Give that stranger a bandage for his head.
We treat visitors here with courtesy – you should know,
you've tested our hospitality to the edge of bankruptcy.

And you've strained my nerves and my heart to breaking
point.
Beyond breaking point.

ANTINOUS
All we want is resolution to this situation . . .

PENELOPE (*cutting through him*)
I've reached a decision.
The morning Odysseus sailed for Troy
he held me by the wrist. Wait for me, he said.
Wait until our baby son is a man with a beard on his chin.
Then for the sake of yourself, for the sake of everything,
choose another man.

That day has come.

TELEMACHUS (*under his breath*)
No, mother.

ODYSSEUS (*hushed*)
Let her speak.

PENELOPE
It's time to . . . give up the ghost.
I'm worn down.
Why you should want me – empty and bitter and cold,
all my womanly beauty drained by grief – Zeus only knows.
But I'll honour my husband's will. I'll marry one of you.

[236]

There is agreement, relief and self-congratulation among the
suitors.

AMPHINOMUS
My lady, gracious queen . . .

PENELOPE
Time was when a suitor would court his lady with
  presents.
Lay wondrous offerings at her feet.
Outbid his rivals with promises of wealth.
Shower the family of the bride-to-be with shimmering
  gifts.

TELEMACHUS (*aside*)
She lines her pockets into the bargain.

ODYSSEUS (*hushed response*)
No, she fleeces them. Let them pay.

ANTINOUS
My lady, your change of heart is most welcome and most
  timely.
And now that common sense has taken hold,
we'll court you the way that tradition demands.
We'll bring gifts. Pile them to the ceiling if need be.

And may the best man win!

The suitors cheer.

PENELOPE
But leave me in peace now.
Go home to your houses – let me have one last night
to prepare, and make my peace, and accept my loss.

AMPHINOMUS
We'll grant you that, of course.

[237]

The suitors begin to pack up their bags and leave the house.

PENELOPE
  Eumaeus?

EUMAEUS
  You call for me, my lady?

PENELOPE
  Come here and answer me a question.

Eumaeus makes his way to Penelope.

  The old man who begged from the table, who is he?

EUMAEUS
  A stranger, shipwrecked coming from Crete,
  washed up on Ithaca's shore.
  He knocked on my door and I took him in.

PENELOPE
  From Crete?
  The trade winds might have whispered my husband's
    name in his ears.
  Tell him to expect my company.
  I'll speak to him in due course.

*

Later. The house of Odysseus stands quiet.

EUMAEUS
  Old man, here she comes. Dust yourself down.

PENELOPE
  Don't stand up – please.
  Those suitors brought shame on this house
  with their rudeness towards you. You deserve to sit.

[238]

ODYSSEUS

All I've heard of your kindness is true. And your beauty.

PENELOPE

Where are you from, stranger?

ODYSSEUS

Lady, don't ask me the name of my country.
Don't ask me to crack open my heart in front of you.
You've troubles enough in this house without my sob-
    story.
I'll weep, and you'll think me drunk and maudlin.

PENELOPE

Nothing could take my spirits any lower.

ODYSSEUS

You've suffered and suffered – your face tells me as much.

PENELOPE

When Odysseus, my husband, sailed for Troy,
he took my soul with him.

Then the vultures started to circle.
I held those suitors off for long enough,
weaving a shroud for my husband's father,
telling them I wouldn't wed until the long fine threads
were interlaced and woven tight.

Then unpicked it every night! For three years it was my
    alibi.

ODYSSEUS

A brilliant scheme.

PENELOPE

But they found me out. The maidservants were two-faced.
Now there's no more web to weave. No escape.

ODYSSEUS
    Lady, you've been honest with me, now I'll say something
        about myself.
    My homeland is Crete.

PENELOPE
    I know of it.

ODYSSEUS
    It was there I met him. Odysseus.

PENELOPE
    You met my husband? How long ago?

ODYSSEUS
    Years and years, I'm afraid.
    He was making for Troy when the wind blew him off
        course.
    He moored in the harbour to escape the storm.
    One evening he ate in my house.
    Then after two weeks, with the wind back to right again,
        he sailed.
    That was the last I saw of him.

PENELOPE
    He ate in your house?

ODYSSEUS
    Sat as close to me as you are sitting right now.

PENELOPE
    If it's true, tell me what clothes he wore?

ODYSSEUS
    Lady, it's difficult. Twenty years – the memory fades.

PENELOPE

No one forgets Odysseus. What did he wear?

ODYSSEUS

Well, let me conjure up the picture of him standing at my
     door.
A blue cloak. No, purple. A purple cloak.

PENELOPE

Go on.

ODYSSEUS

With a double fold – that's right.
A purple cloak with a double fold.
Pinned with a brooch, and on the brooch
the image of a deer or faun,
being dragged to the ground by a dog, a hunting hound.
I admired it. Well, all did.
If I close my eyes I see it clear as daylight now.

PENELOPE (*moved by the account of her husband*)

I gave him that cloak.
I folded it, fastened that pin.
It was the last time I touched him.

ODYSSEUS

I'm sorry to have opened the wound again.

PENELOPE

It never closed.

You gave my husband shelter a long way from home.
It's the least I can do to give you the same. Eurycleia?

EURYCLEIA

Yes, my lady. Coming, my lady.

PENELOPE

Here's our old nurse. She suckled Odysseus himself.

EURYCLEIA
  That I did, my lady. He fed at my breast.

PENELOPE
  Make up a couch for our guest.

EURYCLEIA
  I will.

PENELOPE
  And wash him. Bathe his feet.

ODYSSEUS
  I'm fine here on the hearth rug – I'm used to roughing it.

PENELOPE
  I won't hear of you not being comfortable under my roof.
  And let her bathe your feet – you'll feel better for it.
  I'll be in the upper room. I have prayers to say.

Eurycleia kneels at Odysseus' feet with a bowl of water.

EURYCLEIA
  Come on, off with those sandals.
  My, these feet have squashed some miles under them.
  Not damaged though. Not a nail broken. Good strong
    ankles.

  You're very alike, you know, you and Odysseus.

ODYSSEUS
  People have commented on the resemblance.

EURYCLEIA
  Alike in height and width. Similar voices.
  I thought you were far older, 'scuse me saying,
  but these are a younger man's feet. Same size as his, I'd say.

ODYSSEUS

Have you finished?

EURYCLEIA

I've only just started – relax. Lie back.
He liked his feet bathed, you know.

ODYSSEUS

Did he?

EURYCLEIA

Like washing his troubles away, he'd say.
He had a scar on his leg.

ODYSSEUS

Really?

EURYCLEIA

I'll say he did. Went hunting when he was a lad,
and a wild boar comes tearing out of a thicket.
He killed it with a spear, bang! –
but not before it gouged the flesh with its tusk.

ODYSSEUS

Thank you, you can stop now.

EURYCLEIA

A real gash, it was. Just below the knee.
No, on the other leg, just about there, just . . .

She drops his leg. The bronze bowl of water turns over onto the floor.

EURYCLEIA

All the Gods and all the stars in heaven – it's you.

ODYSSEUS

Be quiet, Eurycleia.

EURYCLEIA
It's my lord and master.
Dear child – it's you, Odysseus. It's Odysseus.

ODYSSEUS (*almost violently*)
Keep it closed, old nurse.
You suckled me into life – don't get me killed now.
This stays a secret until those suitors are dead,
or, as I live and breathe, I'll have to finish you as well,
along with those other servants and maids who've double-
    crossed us.

PENELOPE (*from afar*)
What's going on?

EURYCLEIA
I'll be as silent as a lump of iron.
I'll be as silent as a stone, trapped in a block of ice, buried
    under snow.

ODYSSEUS
See to it.

EURYCLEIA (*hushed, but excited*)
And when your hands have finished with those suitors,
bang! bang! bang!
I'll point out the turncoats in this house.
I'll point them out with my own hand . . .

PENELOPE (*entering*)
Nurse – did you spill the water?
Your old hands are growing weak . . .

ODYSSEUS
No, it was my fault. She soothed me to sleep,
then I kicked out in a dream.

EURYCLEIA

    I'll run and fetch a cloth to mop up the mess.
    And blankets for a bed. Excuse me, ma'am. Sir.

Eurycleia exits.

PENELOPE

    I have a dream – the same dream every night.
    Are you someone who knows the meaning of dreams?

ODYSSEUS

    Dreams are hard to fathom. What happens in yours?

PENELOPE

    I have twenty white geese in the house – pets, really.
    In the dream, an eagle swoops from the sky
    and breaks the neck of every one with its hooked beak.
    What does it mean?

ODYSSEUS

    It's a good sign, isn't it?
    Golden Odysseus will swoop on the house
    and slay the suitors – isn't that what the dream says?

PENELOPE

    I clung to that thought for a long time –
    woke every morning full of hope. But I see now I was
        wrong.
    Now it's a nightmare – I sleep in cold sweat.

    Well, tomorrow waits in the east – an evil day.
    I have an archery contest in mind – what do you think?

ODYSSEUS

    With the winner taking your hand?

PENELOPE
To sort the wheat from the chaff. The men from the boys.

ODYSSEUS
It sounds perfect to me. Appropriate.
Whoever claims you as his prize must be no ordinary
man.

PENELOPE
Goodnight, stranger from Crete.

Penelope leaves.

ODYSSEUS
My lady. My Penelope.

Eurycleia returns.

EURYCLEIA
Here's enough blankets to keep a horse warm.
Need anything else, *stranger*?

ODYSSEUS
Nothing.

EURYCLEIA
Then I'll say goodnight. *Stranger!*

ODYSSEUS
Don't squeal, Eurycleia. Keep the secret.

EURYCLEIA
My lips are stitched together. Mmnnnn!

Odysseus beds down for the night.

ODYSSEUS (*to himself*)
Be strong, Odysseus. Be iron-hearted.
Don't let doubts gnaw away at your courage all night.

ATHENA

   Awake, or talking in your sleep, Odysseus?

ODYSSEUS

   Athena – silver-eyed Goddess.
   I thought . . . I thought you'd deserted me when I most
      needed you.

ATHENA

   Desertion?
   The Gods don't waver – hesitation and doubt are human
      failings.

ODYSSEUS

   Doubt and hesitation are in me tonight.
   There must be fifty suitors at least.
   Do you promise to fight at my shoulder?
   Does almighty Zeus lend his support to this venture?

ATHENA

   Go to the heavy door of your wife's chamber, Odysseus.
   Don't enter – just listen.

ODYSSEUS

   Skulk in the corridors of my house, eavesdropping –
   what kind of plan is that? That's no promise.
   Athena? Athena?

*Odysseus climbs the steps and stands outside Penelope's
chamber. He puts his ear to the door.*

   I hear nothing. The sound of sleeping.

Penelope begins to murmur.

   My wife. Praying. Saying her prayers. A sweet sound.

PENELOPE (*from inside the room*)
    Artemis, hear me.
    Aphrodite, hear me.
    Hera and Athena, all women of Olympus,
    hear this woman's request.

    Take away my life.

ODYSSEUS (*to himself*)
    No, Penelope.

PENELOPE
    Let an arrow fly at my life.
    Let me join my husband in death.
    Sleep was once my escape,
    now dreams worm into my mind.

    Let oblivion draw its dark sheet over me.
    Goddesses of Olympus,
    lay a weight on my heart now, and let me sleep.

ODYSSEUS (*to himself*)
    Athena – you'd have me suffer more,
    listen to my wife pleading for death.

    Well, now doubts and hesitation are blown away.
    Tomorrow I'll rage. Tomorrow I'll flare and blaze.
    Beware those who stand in the blast.
    I come alive – every atom of me ignites now with fury.

THE STRINGING OF THE BOW

The next morning. Loud, boastful and already drinking, the suitors are gathered in the hall for the day of reckoning. Also present in the hall are Telemachus, Eurycleia, Eumaeus and Odysseus, still in disguise.

ODYSSEUS (*under his breath, to Telemachus*)
Did you empty the weapons from the locker and hide
    them?

TELEMACHUS
All hidden out of harm's way.

ODYSSEUS
Remember, do nothing until I give the signal.
The timing is everything.

EURYMACHUS
Telemachus, no hard feelings, eh?
You're not losing a mother. You're gaining a step-father.

The suitors laugh.

TELEMACHUS
A thought that hadn't escaped me, Eurymachus.

ANTINOUS
Don't look so worried. We won't be too hard on you.
But if I'm the chosen one, you'll have to be sent abroad.
Some island with only wolves and bears for company.
Toughen you up.

EURYMACHUS
It's what his father would have wanted.

ANTINOUS
    Exactly. And we must do right by the father
    if we're to step into his boots, slip between his sheets!
    So don't think we'll neglect you, Telemachus.
    On the contrary. What say you, Amphinomus?

AMPHINOMUS
    I won't goad the son of the woman I want to marry.
    But I've got to admit to feeling excited – even giddy.
    Let it happen! I've got a lucky feeling about this day.

EUMAEUS (*making an announcement*)
    The queen will address you.

They carry on talking.

TELEMACHUS
    THE QUEEN WILL ADDRESS YOU. If you're quite
    ready.

They fall silent as Penelope enters the room.

PENELOPE
    Your gifts are stacked high in the lobby.
    They are duly noted.

    But I won't be bought by material goods alone.

EURYMACHUS
    What's this – more time wasting?

EUMAEUS
    Let her finish.

PENELOPE
    A contest. Eumaeus, raise the weapon for all to see.
    This was my husband's bow – a gift from Iphitos.
    He didn't carry it into war but left it here in his house.

Surely you didn't think I'd marry for money alone –
throw myself at the man with the deepest pockets
or the widest fields or the greatest flocks to his name.
The man who takes my husband's place must be strong –
strong enough to lace this heavy bow.
And steady enough to lift it, take aim,
let an arrow pass between those twelve axe-shafts – look –
planted in line for the occasion.
And brave – steely enough to contemplate failure.

So who here has the courage?

EURYMACHUS
    This wasn't the plan. This wasn't what we expected.

TELEMACHUS
    Spontaneity was never your strong point, was it?

EURYMACHUS
    You little runt . . .

TELEMACHUS
    Or you, Antinous? Nothing to say for a change?
    Maybe you haven't got what it takes?
    Maybe you don't have the nerve? The guts? The balls?

ANTINOUS (*keeping cool*)
    This . . . is an unexpected turn of events.

EUMAEUS
    Look at them, blown over by a little change in the breeze.
    They're not fit to marry one of my pigs.

ANTINOUS
    You keep your mouth closed, swineherd.

TELEMACHUS
  None of you? No?
  Then I'll lace it myself. Why not? Eumaeus, pass the bow.

Eumaeus grunts under the weight.

ANTINOUS
  It proves nothing.

TELEMACHUS
  Spoken like a true coward.

EURYMACHUS
  So what will you do if you win – marry your own
    mother?

TELEMACHUS
  Lead her away from you rabble.

He grapples with the bow.

  Look, it already bends.

EURYMACHUS
  You'll give yourself an accident, Telemachus.

TELEMACHUS (*trying to flex the bow*)
  It gives to my strength. It gives and gives.

EUMAEUS
  They say a bow like this only yields to its true owner.

TELEMACHUS
  An inch more. Just an inch more . . .

ODYSSEUS (*under his breath*)
  No, Telemachus. Don't.

The bow finally springs apart in his hands.

EUMAEUS

Hard luck, Telemachus. At least you made the effort.
Your father would have been proud, just as I am.

AMPHINOMUS (*carried away with excitement*)

Move aside.

ANTINOUS

You, Amphinomus. What's this sudden rush of blood to
the head?

AMPHINOMUS

Let me have the next attempt.
I see how it's done.
I'll string the bow and fire through the axes –

I can feel it – this is my moment.
(*He struggles with the bow.*)
Come on, give to me, give to me . . . Damn you!
(*amazed at his inability*)
I . . . couldn't. I really thought . . . Now I'm ashamed of
my failure.

EURYMACHUS

It wasn't in the stars. You've never been lucky,
Amphinomus –
I told you that when we played dice.

AMPHINOMUS (*broken*)

Not my destiny. I wonder what is, then?
I thought the path of my life led to this day.

EURYMACHUS

Give it to me. GIVE IT ME.
I feel a tide of energy.

(*He shouts at the bow.*)
COME ON. BEND, YOU STUBBORN
   CONTRAPTION . . .
(*He fights with the bow, trying to lace the string.*)
BEND FOR ME. I'LL BREAK YOUR SPINE.
I'LL BREAK YOU, YOU . . . NNNGGGNNRRRR.

The bow springs apart again. He throws it aside in disgust.

ODYSSEUS (*plainly*)
   Let me try.

ANTINOUS
   What – is this flea-bag still in the house?
   I thought I'd had you thrown in the gutter.

TELEMACHUS
   It isn't your house. You don't give the orders.

EUMAEUS
   Shall I give him the bow?

ANTINOUS
   Of course not. He's just a drifter, a no-mark.
   This is the contest for the Queen of Ithaca –
   not some shooting gallery at a travelling circus. Kick him
      outside.

PENELOPE
   Give him the bow.

ANTINOUS
   This is farcical.

PENELOPE
   Give him the bow – what is there to lose?
   If he succeeds I'm hardly going to marry him,

but I will kit him out with clothes and a sword for his
    journey.
And the rest of you suitors will be judged by his
    standards.
Give him the bow.

TELEMACHUS
    I sanction it.

PENELOPE
    Quite rightly.

TELEMACHUS
    And now, mother, go to your room.

PENELOPE
    What?
    I will not leave this hall until the outcome of this contest
        is . . .

TELEMACHUS
    You will take instruction from the man of the house!
    I have authority over the bow. I decide.
    Not another word. Go to your room.

*There is a piercing silence, before Penelope turns and walks
away. The door of her bed-chamber is slammed shut.*

    (*to Eumaeus*)
    Hand him the bow.

ODYSSEUS (*hushed, to Eumaeus*)
    Eumaeus, do you believe in Odysseus? Are you loyal to
        his name?

EUMAEUS
    To my dying day. To my dying breath.

ODYSSEUS
Then believe in me. Look in my face. Look at Odysseus.

EUMAEUS (*astonished*)
Master? My master? It can't be.

ODYSSEUS
You'll have the proof soon enough.
Go with Eurycleia. Lock all the doors. Keep my wife in
her room.

ANTINOUS
Well, men, this should be worth watching.
More likely the bow will bend him!

ODYSSEUS
Oh yes, Antinous, you'll find this entertaining all right.

Look, the bow resists. It resists and resists.
Then suddenly . . . it gives.

The suitors are transfixed.

So I lace the length of gut.
(*plucking the bow*)
Listen, taut, like an instrument.
Do you hear that note – the sweet spot?
The sound of power waiting to be unleashed.
So much for strength.
Now steadiness – an arrow from the quiver, and I take
aim.
The trick here is not to flinch, not to blink, not even to
breathe,
then . . .

The arrow passes cleanly between the axes.

AMPHINOMUS
He did it. He did it!
A clean shot – not one of the axes clipped.

EURYMACHUS
Unbelievable.

ODYSSEUS
Telemachus, won't you join me on this platform?

TELEMACHUS
Congratulations, stranger. You have the strength of a bull,
and the steadiness of a rock, and a sniper's eye.

ODYSSEUS
And no fluke either. Look, I'll prove it again.

ANTINOUS
Don't point that thing at me, beggar man.

ODYSSEUS
Oh yes, Antinous. As you lift that glass to your lips
and swallow down a gulp of wine, a moving target
rises and falls in your throat. Your Adam's apple,
    Antinous.
Let the Gods guide this arrow straight to its mark.

*He shoots Antinous in the throat. There is uproar in the
hall. Some men shout that the doors are locked, others
that the weapon cupboards are empty.*

ODYSSEUS
You rabid mongrels. You vermin.
You thought Odysseus would never return.
You fouled my house. Polluted my family. Scandalized my
    name.

EURYMACHUS
  Odysseus, if it's really you, spare us. It was Antinous all
    along,
  his idea, his planning and scheming that kept us here.
  Spare us, Odysseus, you've killed the worst of us.
  That can be our lesson.

ODYSSEUS
  No, Eurymachus, your lesson is more painful to learn.

EURYMACHUS
  We'll give back everything we've taken. Bronze, gold,
  you name it. Just say the price and we'll pay, I promise.

ODYSSEUS
  All the money in the world wouldn't cover it.
  This is the only way your debt can be settled.

He fires an arrow into Eurymachus' chest.

AMPHINOMUS
  Not me, Odysseus. You heard how I spoke out.
  I was never happy with this situation, never comfortable.

TELEMACHUS (*driving a spear into his back*)
  But never as uncomfortable as now I'll bet,
  wearing a spear between your shoulder blades.

The chaos in the hall escalates.

ODYSSEUS (*loosing off arrows left, right and centre*)
  You'll all die. You'll die, and you'll die, and you'll die.
  It's nothing less than you deserve.
  It's better than you deserve!
  (*shouting*)
  And when Death asks who sent you to his gate,
  don't forget my name.
  Tell him ODYSSEUS, ODYSSEUS, ODYSSEUS!

REUNION

Eurycleia goes to Penelope's room. She is sleeping.

EURYCLEIA
  My lady.

PENELOPE (*stirring*)
  Is it over?

EURYCLEIA
  Over, my lady.

PENELOPE
  Over, then. So who shall I marry?

EURYCLEIA
  Ah, there'll be no marriage for them that's already wed.

PENELOPE
  Don't set me a riddle. Just tell me.

EURYCLEIA
  Your husband is here, my lady.

PENELOPE
  You antagonize me, Eurycleia.
  It's only your age that saves you. Go away.

EURYCLEIA
  No, my lady. You insult me. But you're forgiven.

PENELOPE
  What did you say?

EURYCLEIA
  It's a blood-bath down there, but one to savour.

The suitors are dead, slain by Odysseus.
He was the beggar-stranger!
I guessed it but no one else did, not even his wife.
(*suddenly*)
YOU'RE SAVED! GO TO HIM. GO TO HIM.

PENELOPE
You're twisting the knife, Eurycleia. Your mind's gone.
I won't have you in the house if . . .

Odysseus stands in the door. Athena has removed his disguise.

ODYSSEUS
Leave us, Eurycleia.

EURYCLEIA
Yes, master. Excuse me, my lady.
Ha!

Eurycleia leaves the room and a long silence follows.

PENELOPE
It's the height of rudeness to enter a lady's chamber.

ODYSSEUS
You recognize me now that I'm washed and robed.
You know who I am.

PENELOPE
Stranger, I could have you strung up for this impertinence.

ODYSSEUS
You know I'm real, Penelope.

Silence.

It's you who acts the stranger now.

The Gods on Olympus gave you a stubborn heart.
Twenty years I've been away, ten of them fighting a war,
ten more fighting my way back to this chamber, this door.
No other woman would hold back like you.

PENELOPE

Who are you? I don't know who you are.

ODYSSEUS

You know.

PENELOPE

I know very well what my husband looked like when he
    set sail.
But what does he look like now?
You're a stranger. You're unfamiliar. Unknown.

ODYSSEUS

Very well!
I won't set foot inside this sacred room.
I'll sleep outside on the floor. Tell the maid to make up a
    bed.

PENELOPE

Wait a moment. Wait, let me think.
You should be honoured for what you have done for us.
You should . . . sleep in his bed.

ODYSSEUS

Oh, recognition at last!

PENELOPE

But not in my room. Drag the bed outside –
this bed that Odysseus built.

ODYSSEUS (*in anger and confusion*)
What? What do you want me to do?
That bed won't budge an inch. It's not furniture,
it's carved from the bole of an olive tree.
Its branches were stripped, it was planed flat,
stones were set in its wood, doors were added
and posts and a canopy over the top, its grain
was inlaid with silver and gold thread.

It wasn't carried here from a carpenter's shed,
that bed still has roots in the ground.

This room was built around that bed.

That marriage bed is the corner-stone of the whole house.

Penelope begins to weep

I shouldn't have raised my voice.

PENELOPE
Odysseus.

ODYSSEUS
I shouldn't have . . . I'll keep away . . .

PENELOPE
Only my husband knows the truth about this bed.
Only my husband. Oh Odysseus, my Odysseus.

They embrace and weep.

Come to me, Odysseus. Don't hate my stubbornness.
How should a woman know a man after twenty years?
How should a wife know her husband after that long?
Impostors have come here, men pretending to be you.
But no one has come close, Odysseus, do you hear?
It's only my stubborn heart that has kept us alive.

Only two people know the secret of this bed.

ODYSSEUS

This bed that I built – it proves who I am.

PENELOPE

And proves my faithfulness.

ODYSSEUS

And proves my trust.
And proves my heart, which ached all these endless years.

PENELOPE

You're home now, my Odysseus.

ODYSSEUS

You are my home, Penelope. You are my Ithaca.

OLYMPUS

ZEUS

You fought like a warrior, Athena. Like you were born
  to it.

ATHENA

It gave me no pleasure. It was a just cause.

ZEUS

And nobody saw you? Nobody went to the Kingdom of
  the Dead
wearing a picture of your face in his eyes?

ATHENA

I was invisible – at Odysseus' side.

I lent an unseen hand when he laced the bow,
bent that obstinate wood into shape.

And I flew when the first arrow was fired,
guided it smartly into Antinous' hollow throat.
His eyes stared. Stunned and wordless,
he buckled at the knees. Blood spouted from his nose.

Eurymachus took the next quill. I carried its flight
between my finger and thumb,
felt it shatter the cage of his ribs,
tear into his hollow chest.

Then I stood behind Telemachus' bronze-headed spear,
and when timid Amphinomus pleaded for his life
I drove it home into his hollow lungs.

I had a silent hand in every suitor's death.

ZEUS

It's how justice should be: an invisible, silent force.

ATHENA

And like love too. Love should be the same.

ZEUS

Come here.

ATHENA

My father . . .

ZEUS

You have a speck of blood on your face.

ATHENA

I'll . . . go and wash.

ZEUS

Wait, Athena, you have one more task.

It's night-time on Ithaca.
Look, curtains are drawn in the bed-chamber of husband
  and wife.

Give those lovers the longest night of their lives.
Go to the dawn in the east and hold it back by its edge.
Don't let darkness roll up its blanket just yet.
Don't let the morning saddle its clattering horses to the
  sun.

There'll be other days. And more tragedy for that house, I
  expect –
no hero ever goes quietly into old age.
But let them have their night of all nights.
In privacy. Out of sight.

Now, bring the clouds together in gentle thunder over the
   earth
and close this human story from our God-like eyes.

Thunder reverberates over Ithaca.